A Good Teacher
in Every Classroom

The National Academy
of Education
Committee
on Teacher Education

Linda Darling-Hammond
Joan Baratz-Snowden
Editors

A Good Teacher in Every Classroom

Preparing the Highly Qualified Teachers Our Children Deserve

JOSSEY-BASS
A Wiley Imprint
www.josseybass.com

Published by Jossey-Bass
A Wiley Imprint
989 Market Street, San Francisco, CA 94103-1741   www.josseybass.com

This book draws in part upon the work *Preparing Teachers for a Changing World: What
Teachers Should Learn and Be Able to Do*, edited by Linda Darling-Hammond and John
Bransford, published by Jossey-Bass.

Jossey-Bass books and products are available through most bookstores. To contact Jossey-Bass
directly call our Customer Care Department within the U.S. at 800-956-7739, outside the
U.S. at 317-572-3986, or fax 317-572-4002.

Jossey-Bass also publishes its books in a variety of electronic formats. Some content that
appears in print may not be available in electronic books.

Library of Congress Cataloging-in-Publication Data

A good teacher in every classroom : preparing the highly qualified teachers our children
deserve / The National Academy of Education, Committee on Teacher Education ;
Linda Darling-Hammond, Joan Baratz-Snowden, eds.
    p. cm.
  Includes bibliographical references and index.
  ISBN-13 978-0-7879-7466-4 (alk. paper)
  ISBN-10 0-7879-7466-8 (alk. paper)
  1. Teachers—Training of—United States. I. Darling-Hammond, Linda, date. II. Baratz-
Snowden, Joan C. III. National Academy of Education. Committee on Teacher Education.
  LB1715.G516 2005
  370'.71'1—dc22   2005003695

Printed in the United States of America
FIRST EDITION
PB Printing   10 9 8 7 6 5 4 3 2 1

The Jossey-Bass Education Series

Contents

Preface and
Acknowledgments

At some point in their development, all professions have worked to achieve consensus about the key elements of a professional curriculum: the building blocks of preparation for all entrants into an occupation. In medicine this happened at the turn of the twentieth century following the release of the Flexner report that critiqued the uneven quality of medical education (Flexner & Pritchett, 1910). Efforts to create a common curriculum for legal education followed shortly thereafter. Fields such as engineering and architecture turned to this work in the mid-1900s.

In similar fashion, over the last two decades the teaching profession has begun to codify its knowledge base for professional practice and to establish standards for the work of practitioners. This work has been made possible by large strides in our understanding of student learning and teaching practices that support it. This volume, sponsored by the National Academy of Education, builds on these prior efforts and takes up the question of how this understanding—combined with a growing base of knowledge about how *teachers* learn—can inform the education of teachers.

The National Academy's Committee on Teacher Education includes scholars and researchers, practicing teachers, and teacher educators with wide-ranging expertise. The recommendations in this volume are based on research about learning, effective teaching, teacher learning, and teacher education. In addition to conducting reviews of research regarding children's learning, development, assessment, teaching, and other domains, the committee drew on the knowledge and experience of its members and of representatives of a group of cooperating universities—the City University of New York, Dillard University, Indiana State University, New York University, Stanford University, University of Georgia, University of Texas–El Paso, and Xavier University—who provided grounded feedback about the committee's recommendations.

This volume is one of the products of the committee's work. It outlines core concepts and strategies that should inform initial teacher preparation, whether it is delivered in traditional or alternative settings, and policies needed to assure that all teachers can gain access to this knowledge. The recommendations of this volume focus not on what current preparation programs generally deliver to prospective teachers, but rather on what teachers need to know and do to ensure that all their students learn. A more comprehensive treatment of these issues, including the research on which the recommendations are based, is included in the committee's major report, *Preparing Teachers for a Changing World: What Teachers Should Learn and Be Able to Do*. A companion volume, *Knowledge to Support the Teaching of Reading: Preparing Teachers for a Changing World*, examines the implications for teacher education of knowledge for teaching reading.

The work of the committee was funded by the Office of Educational Research and Improvement in the U.S. Department of Education, under grant number R215U000018, and by the Ford Foundation. While we are grateful for the support of these funders, this work does not represent the opinions of these agencies.

The committee is also grateful to Robert Floden, Michael Fullan, Sonia Nieto, and Seymour Sarason for very helpful reviews of the research volume on which this report is based, and to Maureen Hallinan, who skillfully served as moderator of that volume on behalf of the Academy. Finally, we appreciate the efforts of the many other teachers and teacher educators who contributed to this work and who daily engage in the work of teaching and learning. We hope, most of all, that this effort contributes to their important work.

Committee on Teacher Education, National Academy of Education

Committee Co-chairs

John Bransford, University of Washington

Linda Darling-Hammond, Stanford University

Committee Members

James Banks, University of Washington

Joan Baratz-Snowden, American Federation of Teachers

David Berliner, Arizona State University

Marilyn Cochran-Smith, Boston College

James Comer, Yale University

Sharon Derry, University of Wisconsin-Madison

Emily Feistrizer, National Center for Education Information

Edmund Gordon, Teachers College, Columbia University

Pamela Grossman, Stanford University

Cris Gutierrez, Los Angeles Unified School District

Frances Degan Horowitz, The City University of New York

Evelyn Jenkins-Gunn, Pelham Memorial High School

Carol Lee, Northwestern University

Cooperating University Liaisons

Diana Quatroche, Indiana State University

Frances Rust, New York University

Linda Darling-Hammond, Stanford University

Michael Padilla, University of Georgia

Rosalind Hale, Xavier University

Arturo Pacheco, University of Texas, El Paso

Nicholas Michelli, City University of New York

Kassie Freeman, Dillard University

Staff

Helen Duffy

Karen Hammerness

Pamela LePage

A Good Teacher
in Every Classroom

Introduction

Each fall, more than one hundred thousand new teachers enter classrooms across America. Some enter with strong preparation, competent and confident to help their students learn. Many, however, are unprepared to meet the challenges they face. The beginning teachers who enter U.S. schools in growing numbers each year vary greatly in the skills and experiences they bring to the job and the formal preparation they have been given to assume the demanding responsibility of educating America's youth. Most are recent college graduates who have gone through a formal teacher education program. A growing number are career switchers with widely varying preparation—from a few weeks to a year or more. Some teachers hired on emergency permits have had no preparation at all. Tens of thousands of new teachers, especially in low-income urban and rural areas, have had little or no exposure to basic information about children, curriculum, or schools. And too many of those who have gone through a teacher education program have not received a rigorous education in some of the essential knowledge and clinical training that would prepare them for success in the classroom.

Why is this the case? How is it that we permit so many ill-prepared individuals to assume such an important role in society? And why do we let some of the least prepared teach our most needy children in the most difficult circumstances? There are many answers to these questions, including at least the following:

- As a society, we do not invest seriously in the lives of children, most especially poor children and children of color, who receive the least-prepared teachers.
- The conventional view of teaching is simplistic: teaching is viewed merely as proceeding through a set curriculum in a manner that transmits information from the teacher to the child.
- Many people do not understand what successful teaching requires and do not see teaching as a difficult job that requires rigorous training.
- Others believe that there is not much more to teaching than knowing the subject matter that children should learn.
- Many state licensing systems reflect these attitudes and have entry requirements that compromise standards, especially for teachers who teach poor and minority students.
- Researchers and teacher educators have only recently come to consensus about what is necessary, basic knowledge for entering the classroom and about how such knowledge and skill can be acquired.

Although there are many reasons current teachers are not always well prepared, we have learned a great deal about the importance of good teaching and about what effective teachers do. Far from the popular image of the teacher standing at the front of the room lecturing from a textbook and giving a quiz at the end of the week, we now know that teachers whose students demonstrate strong achievement do much more. Effective teachers use many different tools to assess *how* their students learn as well as *what* the students know. They use this information to help all students advance from where they are to where they need to be. They carefully organize activities, materials, and instruction based on students' prior knowledge and level of development so that all students can be successful. They know what conceptions students bring with them about the subject and what misconceptions are likely to cause them confusion—and they design their lessons to overcome these misinterpretations. They adapt the curriculum to different students' needs; for example, making content more accessible for students who are still learning English and for those who have special educational needs.

Effective teachers engage students in active learning—debating, discussing, researching, writing, evaluating, experimenting, and constructing models, papers, and products in addition to listening to and reading information, watching demonstrations, and practicing skills. They make their expectations for high-quality work very clear, and they provide models of student work that meets those standards. They also provide constant feedback that helps students improve as they continuously revise their work toward these standards. They design and manage a well-functioning, respectful classroom that allows students to work productively. Finally, they involve parents in the learning process and help create strong connections between home and school so that students have fewer obstacles and more supports for their learning. And they do all of this while collaborating with other teachers and administrators to create a seamless curriculum and a supportive environment throughout the school.

Clearly, there is much more to effective teaching than standing in the front of the room giving information to students. And there is much that teachers need to learn in order to do this complex job well. We outline here what teachers need to know before they enter the classroom and what supports they need when they first enter to ensure their development into the effective teachers described above.

The Focus and Organization of This Report

Although we know a great deal more than we once did about how people learn and how to teach effectively, much of this knowledge is only haphazardly available to those who most need it to do their work—the teachers who today are charged with enabling students to reach the highest standards of accomplishment ever envisioned for the full range of students in our nation's schools.

This volume focuses on the preparation of new teachers. It is based on a longer volume sponsored by the National Academy of Education, *Preparing Teachers for a Changing World: What Teachers*

Should Learn and Be Able to Do,[1] which summarizes research on learning, teaching, and teacher education. Drawing on the recommendations of that volume, we offer in this report a set of core ideas, skills, and dispositions that are essential for beginning teachers to acquire. We

- Present what beginning teachers need to know in order to enter the classroom
- Describe best practices for acquiring that knowledge, and
- Lay out the policies needed to assure that beginning teachers can adequately serve the very first students they teach

In addition to describing the core concepts and skills teachers should learn, we discuss how this core knowledge can be acquired, taking into account the different experiences of the teacher candidate pool and the diverse routes for preparing teachers. While acknowledging that it takes many years of experience to develop sophisticated expertise, we focus on the initial preparation that will allow candidates to practice responsibly with the full range of students they first teach and enable them to continue learning on the job and from their peers. We address initial preparation programs of all kinds, including traditional undergraduate and graduate teacher education programs and alternative programs designed for recruits who prepare in post-baccalaureate programs based in universities or school districts. Our focus is not on the format, length, or location of teacher education but on its substance: what beginning teachers need to learn and how they may best be enabled to learn it.

Chapter One

What Do Teachers Need to Know?

Specifying what teachers need to know and be able to do is not a simple task. As is true with all professions—including medicine, the law, and the clergy—there is no one right way to behave as a teacher. Some effective teachers are charismatic whereas others are more retiring. Some are emotional and some are reserved. Some appear stern while others appear more nurturing. There are many different ways that professionals can vary and still be highly effective. Within this variation, however, there are common practices that draw on shared understanding of how to foster student learning.

Our review of the research suggests that the common practices of effective teachers draw on three general areas of knowledge that beginning teachers must acquire in order to be successful with their students (Figure 1.1). These include

- Knowledge of *learners* and how they learn and develop within social contexts
- Understanding of the *subject matter* and skills to be taught in light of the social purposes of education
- Understanding of *teaching* in light of the content and learners to be taught, as informed by assessment and supported by a productive classroom environment

Teaching is complex and the various kinds of knowledge about teaching, learning, and subject matter are interdependent. As professionals, teachers make a commitment to learn what they need to know to help all students succeed. A professional teacher can no

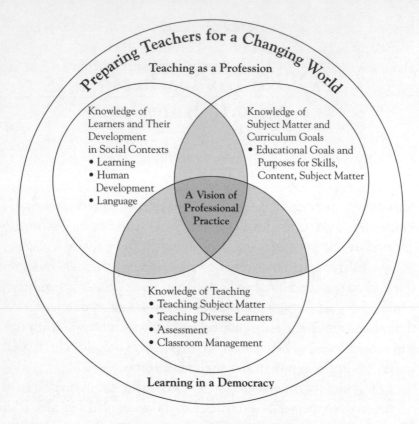

**Figure 1.1. A Framework for
Understanding Teaching and Learning.**

longer naïvely assert, "I taught a great lesson, but nobody 'got it.'"
Teaching, as John Dewey once remarked, is like selling commodi-
ties—they are not sold if nobody buys them. And a teacher has not
taught if no one learns. The vision of professional teaching depicted
in Figure 1.1 connects teaching with student learning and requires
that teachers be able to point to evidence of that learning. It also requires that teachers be mindful of what it means to educate students
within a democracy so that, as citizens, they can participate fully in
political, civic, and economic life.

We use the framework in Figure 1.1 to describe the knowledge
beginning teachers need to acquire in order to be successful with
their students. We base these recommendations on research about

how people learn and what effective teachers understand and do to help them learn. We describe what beginning teachers need to know about learning, human development, language, curriculum, teaching subject matter, teaching diverse learners, assessment, and classroom management.

Knowledge of Learners and Their Development

The first circle in Figure 1.1 addresses the knowledge and skills teachers must have about learners and their learning, development, and language acquisition.

Learning

First and foremost, beginning teachers should understand how children learn. A seminal work for understanding this vast body of research is the National Academy of Sciences report *How People Learn: Brain, Mind, Experiences, and School*.[1] It looks at how children learn from the vantage point of

- The *learner* and his or her strengths, interests, and preconceptions
- The *knowledge*, skills, and attitudes we want children to acquire and how they may be organized so that students can use and transfer what they've learned
- The *assessment* of learning that reveals learning, makes students' thinking visible, and, through feedback, guides further learning
- The *community* within which learning occurs, both within and outside the classroom

What does this mean for what beginning teachers must know? Clearly, teachers must learn to plan for and integrate all four components of this learning framework. Understanding the *learner and the learning process* includes understanding how children develop and learn, as well as how to build on their experiences and cultural backgrounds in making connections to the material. Beginning teachers need to understand

- The constructive *nature of knowing*—the fact that we all actively attempt to interpret our world based on our existing skills, knowledge, and developmental levels. This means that teachers need to understand what students already know and believe and be able to build bridges between students' prior experience and new knowledge. This includes anticipating student misunderstandings in particular areas so that they can be addressed.
- *Cognitive processing*—how people attend to, perceive, and process information, retain it in short- and long-term memory, and retrieve it. This includes understanding the importance of organizing information so that it can be connected to other ideas, incorporated into a schema for learning new information, and retrieved when needed.
- *Metacognition*—how people learn to monitor and regulate their own learning and thinking. This includes knowing how to teach students to think about what they understand, what they need to learn, and what strategies they can use to acquire the information they need.
- *Motivation*—what encourages students to become and remain engaged with their learning. This includes knowing what kinds of tasks, supports, and feedback encourage students to put forth effort and strive to improve.

Furthermore, if they are to support learning that prepares students for life in a complex world, teachers have to consider the *knowledge* they are trying to transmit. In addition to decisions about what is taught, which may be guided by national, state, and local standards, teachers must consider how specific topics and ideas may best be taught. This requires knowledge of the structure of the discipline—how it is organized and what its central concepts are—as well as how to represent these ideas so they can be understood by learners at different ages and stages.

Teachers need to know how to help learners develop a mental map of the domain they are studying—whether it is World War I, the concept of ratio, or how to write an essay—so they can see how ideas are related to one another. Teachers also need to be able to choose vivid examples and representations of the ideas they are teaching that connect to what students already know. Often these examples need to confront directly the misconceptions the students already hold based on their prior experiences. And teachers need to know how to "scaffold" learning by providing just enough of the right kind of assistance at each step to move students forward in their understanding and performance.

Beginning teachers must be able to connect their understanding of *knowledge* with their understanding of *learners* by being *assessment-centered*. Assessment allows teachers to figure out how to pursue their curriculum goals in ways that will work for the students they teach. Assessments, and the feedback they can provide, are actually another source of learning, not just an evaluation of it. Teachers need to know how to construct, select, and use formal and informal assessment tools to show them *how* students are learning and *what* they know, so that they can give constructive feedback that guides further learning and informs instruction.

Finally, learning is influenced by the way people interact in the classroom as well as the home and broader *community*. Teachers need to know how to create information-rich classrooms and social networks where students can learn from each other and the materials in the environment. They need to build upon the "funds of knowledge" that exist in their students' communities and link their students' prior experiences outside of school to those within the classroom.

Human Development

Understanding children, how they develop, and how they learn is critical for effective instruction. Teachers' knowledge of development enables them to be effective in managing the classroom, selecting appropriate tasks, guiding the learning process, and maintaining children's motivation to learn. Without this kind of knowledge, teachers often choose inappropriate learning tasks that bore or frustrate students or that fail to support learning. Developmentally inappropriate tasks not only breed academic failure for students, they also undermine motivation and encourage disruptive behavior.

In order to understand and support students' learning, a teacher must be able to take a "developmental perspective." This includes an understanding that development occurs along a number of different pathways—physical, social, emotional, cognitive, and linguistic, among others. Teachers need to know how to support development along all of the pathways to move children forward in their learning, and they need to understand how these dimensions interact with each other. Teachers particularly need to understand that various stages of development do not necessarily occur at the same age for each child and that development in different dimensions does not necessarily occur evenly within the same child. Teachers with such a perspective understand that students will have different developmental needs and will be able to figure out how to help children learn the right things at the right times in the right ways to maximize their progress.

In order to plan instruction, teachers need to understand general developmental progressions, as well as individual differences in development, so that they are able to determine when children are prepared to learn specific things in particular ways and how to support them as they take on new tasks. In addition to understanding the stages of development—from concrete to more abstract thinking, for example—teachers need to understand the components of tasks they assign and what those tasks require so that they can choose tasks that students are ready to tackle and can provide instruction that addresses what students need to know to succeed.

To do this, teachers must be able to observe students carefully to evaluate not only what they know but also how they learn and perform. Teachers who are able to evaluate a child's developmental level create tasks that address the things the child is ready to learn next, and provide the necessary supports for learning that help children confront new challenges with confidence and growing competence. With that knowledge teachers can help young children continue to feel successful and inspired to learn; without it, they can stymie children's immediate learning and endanger their future success.

Teachers also need to understand how instruction can support development. The older belief that development proceeds at a strict pace that determines children's "readiness" for learning has been replaced with an understanding that learning can affect development, and teachers can construct experiences that advance development. For example, by providing a language-rich classroom with lots of opportunities for speaking, listening, and seeing and using print, students who have had less experience with different kinds of language will develop linguistically and become more ready to learn specific reading skills. With the right support, students can successfully learn to do things that are one level more advanced than what they already understand.

The fact that learning affects development (and vice versa), and that both learning and development are deeply embedded in cultural contexts, means that teachers must understand and appreciate the variety of ways children's experiences can differ and be able to see and build upon personal experiences and cultural strengths if they are to help all students succeed. Understanding children's cultural and home experiences also reduces the opportunities for miscommunication and unnecessary misunderstandings.

Finally, beginning teachers need to understand how to help students build healthy identities as learners and contributors, as well as individuals with solid values and character, since these identities determine how students behave and how they invest their time and effort. When children see themselves as able to succeed if they put forth effort, they are more likely to work hard and help themselves and others. Supporting this kind of development is much easier when all of the adults in the school and home are working together to create a network of common values and support. Thus, teachers should know how to work with parents and colleagues to create common ground for supporting children's development and learning together.

Language

All teachers, regardless of the language backgrounds of their students, are directly and intimately involved with language. No matter what subjects they teach, and whether they work with kindergartners, middle school students, or high school students, teachers use language in many ways in all of their teaching activities. Teachers use language to get students' attention, present information, emphasize particular points, provoke discussion, praise, push for better answers, explain, and sometimes reprimand. For most teachers, however, language use is almost completely unconscious. Few notice the choices that they make in using particular strategies to convey tone or meaning, or recall how they acquired these strategies. Although they are proficient in the use of language, they are unlikely to know how to support language learning without explicit training in how students acquire language skills.

There are a number of big ideas that beginning teachers must understand about language and language differences:

- Speakers of English, like speakers of every other language, use many different varieties or dialects, depending on their regional and class origins.
- These varieties of English, which vary in pronunciation, vocabulary, and even grammatical structures, are all complex and contain sophisticated rules. Depending on the variety spoken, "ain't ain't no error." Instead its use represents the learning of complex rules by its speakers. Teachers will want to help students learn to speak and write standard English in ways that are accepted by the general society. At the same time, it is important for teachers to realize that use of terms like "ain't" signals a response to community conventions rather than a lack of intelligence, and is the result of sophisticated implicit learning rather than the result of some failure to learn.
- Most children come to school as competent speakers of the language spoken in their homes and communities even if that language is not a "standard" variant of English.

• Like speakers of all other languages, speakers of any variant of English—standard or otherwise—use many different registers and styles in their everyday lives. Whatever variety of English they use, children speak differently when addressing their intimate friends than when addressing authority figures such as a teacher or a religious leader. They use language differently at home, in school, on the playground, and elsewhere. Teachers who understand this can help students expand their repertoire to include the styles of various academic conventions, such as a written paper or oral presentation, without asking students to abandon styles appropriate for other contexts, such as seeking advice from a teacher or socializing with a friend.

• Only children whose families use language in ways that are very similar to the ways it is used in school will have acquired the rules for using school-like language. Children who have not been exposed to such language use may initially have difficulty with the many different meanings that questions and other communications have in school settings and will have to be taught these new forms, as well as new vocabulary.

As a foundation for helping students develop language, teachers need to understand the building blocks of language, including the sound system (phonology), the structure of words (morphology), and the structure of sentences (syntax). They need to understand first and second language acquisition (both at home and at school), language variation, and the relationship between language and literacy and to study these topics in relation to classroom practice.

For most children, enhancing language development will involve expanding their linguistic repertoires so that they learn how students are expected to speak and write in school in order to discuss ideas, understand texts, and demonstrate their learning in individual, small group, and large group situations. In the classroom, this means that students who come from language and literacy backgrounds different from those dominant in school will need additional opportunities for practice and feedback in using language for academic purposes in ways consistent with the expectations of schools. For both first- and second-language speakers, teachers need to know how to provide explicit modeling and instruction in how to ask and answer certain kinds of questions, raise points, seek information and clarification, and use technical language in a discipline.

For non-native English speakers, beginning teachers need to understand the importance of providing children opportunities to interact frequently with fluent speakers of English in addition to providing direct instruction in English. They should know how to carry out formal and informal assessments of their English language learners (ELL) to see whether they can follow a class explanation, understand the instructions on a work sheet, read assignments in the time allotted, and the like. Beginning teachers need to know how to evaluate the accessibility of specific lessons for different ELL students (as well as for native English-speaking students) and design ways to provide greater access to the lesson without compromising academic content and language. They need to know how, for example, to appropriately choose and explicitly teach vocabulary, use carefully selected texts, and incorporate graphic representations of ideas. They also need to know how to assess student knowledge of content in ways that do not penalize English language learners for their limitations in oral and written English production. And they need to know how to provide many models of both written and spoken language in the discipline for students to emulate. As they explain how to write a lab report, model a good classroom presentation, or give instruction in reading word problems, teachers will foster the development of academic language for all of the students in their classrooms.

Knowledge of Subject Matter and Curriculum Goals

In addition to understanding learners, teachers must know the subject matter they will teach and understand how to organize curriculum in light of both students' needs and the schools' learning objectives. A "curricular vision"—one that also takes into account the social purposes of education in a democracy—is necessary to guide decisions about what to teach and why. It is what enables teachers to select, adapt, and design materials and lessons so that they can accomplish their goals.

Within the classroom, beginning teachers must be able to plan and enact a set of learning opportunities that provide access to key concepts and skills for all students and help them develop along the various developmental pathways discussed earlier (cognitive, social, linguistic, and so on). The capacity to plan instruction so that it meets the needs of students and the demands of content—and therefore is purposeful and "adds up" to important, well-developed abilities for students—is not something that most people know how to do intuitively or that they learn from unguided classroom experience. Even when teachers are provided with texts and other materials for their classrooms, they must still figure out how to use these to meet goals and standards, given the particular needs and prior learning experiences of their students and the resources and demands of their communities. Based on the learning needs of their students, teachers must make a wide variety of curriculum decisions, ranging from the evaluation and selection of materials to the design and sequencing of tasks, assignments, and activities to the assessment of learning to guide further teaching.

These demands on teachers have grown with the advent of standards-based reforms that presume that teachers will use data about student learning to help students acquire skills they have missed or are struggling to learn. To guide curriculum decisions, beginning teachers must know about national, state, and local standards for student learning. In order to interpret and use these standards, teachers need to be able to identify central concepts that are essential building blocks for understanding, evaluate what their students know, and organize their instruction around critical topics in ways that are appropriate for the particular students they teach.

Beginning teachers' initial knowledge of curriculum also should include an understanding of how to develop and carry out coherent curricular plans in which goals are clear and well-reflected in activities and assessments, and learning experiences are well-designed to achieve the goals. They should know how to make sound curricular decisions, including selecting appropriate materials and choosing teaching strategies that will help students understand key ideas. In today's world, teachers must be able to incorporate the use of technology to help their students access information and resources, develop skills, and represent ideas.

Teachers also need to be able to balance the many curriculum goals that always compete for time and attention so that they are advancing students' in-depth understanding of critical concepts, their ability to make connections among ideas, and their social skills for working with others and contributing to society. And beginning teachers must be aware of age-old curriculum concerns that require continual attention: balancing breadth and depth, incorporating both cognitive and affective goals for learning, avoiding fragmentation, and striving for both relevance and rigor.

As they do this balancing, teachers should be aware of the various purposes of schools, ranging from building academic skills and preparing students vocationally to developing the civic responsibility required of citizens in a democracy and developing the personal talents of individuals. They should also be aware of their professional responsibilities to children and families, including policies regarding curriculum, teaching, and assessment; student rights to an education (for special needs students and language minority students, as well as others); child protection and welfare; and access to particular programs or services for students.

In sum, beginning teachers need to have a sense of where they are going, why they want students to go there, and how they and their students are going to get there. They must be able to create a coherent curriculum that is responsive to the needs of students and construct a classroom community in which the "hidden curriculum" fosters respectful relationships and equitable opportunities to learn.

Knowledge of Teaching

The third circle in Figure 1.1 involves the skillful teaching that enables learners to access the curriculum. In addition to knowledge of subject matter, at least four areas of knowledge and skill are essential for this process: the development of pedagogical content knowledge specific to the subject area, knowledge of how to teach diverse learners, knowledge of assessment, and an understanding of how to manage classroom activities so that students can work purposefully and productively. We turn to each of these below.

Teaching Subject Matter

Much of teaching relies upon anticipating and preparing for student understanding ahead of time. Being prepared to teach subject matter requires deep knowledge of the content itself, the process for learning this content, and the nature of student thinking, reasoning, understanding, and performance within a subject area. These are the foundations of pedagogical content knowledge: the particular knowledge teachers must have to make content accessible to students.

Teachers need flexible understanding of subject matter; they need to know how to solve the problems they pose to students and to know that there are multiple approaches to solving many problems. But such competence is not enough, teachers also must be able to anticipate and respond to typical student patterns of understanding and misunderstanding within a content area. They must know how to anticipate and diagnose such misunderstandings and how to deal with them when they arise. (For an example see Exhibit 1.1.) They should be able to create multiple examples and representations of key ideas that make the content accessible to a wide range of learners. These representations need to connect new ideas that are unfamiliar to things that students already know and have experienced.

Teachers need to understand the processes of learning within a specific field; for example, how do people generally acquire the

**Exhibit 1.1. An Example of
Pedagogical Content Knowledge.**

Imagine you are a second grade teacher working with a small group of children reading a short fairy tale. Concerned about Juan's reading, you take him aside and ask him to read the following short section of the fairy tale aloud. "Once upon a time, an old man and his wife lived in a little house in the woods. They were very poor. The man was going to cut wood for the fire. His wife gave him a little rice cake to take with him. It was the last bit of food they had."

Juan reads: "Once upon a time, an ol man and his wif lived in a little hus in the wuds. They were very poor. the man was going to cut wud for the fir. His wif gave him a little ras cak to tak with him. It was the last bit of f. f. f. food they had."

As Juan's teacher, which two of the following would be most important for you to focus on during instruction?

- Work on high-frequency sight words
- Practice with reading for meaning
- Instruction on CVCe patterns
- Work on consonant sounds
- Use of background knowledge

Based on this sample of Juan's reading, a skilled teacher would observe that this brief segment of text is at Juan's frustration level for reading, and is therefore inappropriate for independent reading. The number and type of errors Juan makes support the need to provide him with easier text. Although it is difficult to get a firm understanding of Juan's strengths and needs from a text at his frustration level, a skilled teacher could learn that Juan's performance indicates that he is not reading for meaning. In the very first sentence, he misreads several words (wife, woods, house) and substitutes nonsense words for them (wif, hus). This suggests that he not only has difficulty decoding these words but that he does not recognize that his guesses do not make sense in the sentence. It does not appear that Juan self-monitors his reading or uses the context to re-read for meaning.

Although it seems as if Juan has not yet learned that reading should make sense, this conclusion is complicated by the fact that Juan is an English language learner. From the information provided, we do not know his level of English proficiency and we have no way of knowing if the words he misreads (wife, house, fire, etc.) are a part of his English listening or speaking vocabulary. It is also complicated by the fact that the passage is at his frustration level, where he misreads many words, making it more difficult to for him to use context to aid in self-monitoring, an issue the teacher would want to explore further.

A skilled teacher would also notice that many of the words that Juan misreads are CVCe words—words that follow the pattern of consonant, vowel, consonant, followed by a silent e. The CVCe generalization, familiar to most experienced readers of English, is that words of this pattern (wife, bite, kite, mate, etc.) generally have a long vowel sound; without the "e" at the end, the vowel becomes short (bit, kit, mat, etc.). Juan pronounces the consonant sounds correctly, but mispronounces the medial vowels in these words as short vowel sounds. He has not yet learned the orthographic pattern that signals a long vowel sound. A knowledgeable teacher would target this for instruction to help Juan improve his ability to decode text and then begin to read for meaning.

Source: This example is drawn from Sheila Valencia, University of Washington, and is included in Pamela Grossman and Alan Schoenfeld, "Teaching Subject Matter," in *Preparing Teachers for a Changing World: What Teachers Should Learn and Be Able to Do.* San Francisco: Jossey-Bass, 2005.

critical concepts, thinking skills, and performance abilities that are needed to become a proficient mathematician, reader, writer, scientist, historian, artist, musician, or language speaker? They also need to understand the structure of the discipline: what the major ideas and modes of inquiry are that distinguish the discipline, for example, experimentation in science, perspective and evidence in history and social science, meaning and expression in the language arts, logic and problem solving in mathematics, and so on.

Beginning teachers should be able to answer the following questions about the teaching of their subject area(s):

- *How do we define the subject matter?* What are the central concepts and processes involved in knowing the subject matter? Are there competing definitions of the subject matter? How do national and state standards or frameworks define the content and what it means to know the content?

- *What are the different purposes for teaching the subject matter?* Why is the subject important for students to study? What aspects of the subject are most important? Are there different purposes for teaching the subject matter depending upon the age of students?

- *What does understanding or strong performance look like with regard to this subject matter?* What are the different aspects of understanding and performance? What are students likely to understand about the subject matter at different developmental stages? How do student understanding and proficiency develop, and how can instruction support this development?

- *What are the primary curricula available to teach the subject matter?* What definitions of the subject are embedded within the curriculum materials? How are curricula aligned with national and state standards? How are they articulated across grade levels? How can teachers use curriculum materials effectively to support student learning?

- *How can teachers assess student understanding and performance within a subject matter domain?* What tools are most useful for assessing student competence? How do teachers use the results of these assessments to inform instruction?

- *What are the practices that characterize the teaching of particular content?* What practices and approaches have been shown to be effective in promoting student learning? Are there practices that are particularly effective with specific groups of learners? What representations, examples, and analogies are particularly useful in helping students grasp particular concepts or ideas?

Teaching Diverse Learners

In today's schools, teachers must be prepared to teach a diverse student population. Students of color now comprise 40 percent of elementary and secondary students, and more than 10 percent of students are recent immigrants who are new English language learners. In addition to a wide range of language and cultural backgrounds, diversity in the range of academic abilities within classrooms has also grown as more students with exceptional needs are mainstreamed. Of the 13 percent of students identified for special education, half spend most of their time in general education classrooms. Beginning teachers must be prepared to take into account the different experiences and academic needs of a wide range of students as they plan and teach.

To teach all children well, teachers must know how to tailor their curriculum and instruction so that their students will be engaged in meaningful work. A basic principle of learning is that people need to begin with what they already know and have experienced and connect it to new information or ideas they are trying to learn. Thus, beginning teachers need to know how to learn about their students' experiences in order to construct curriculum and teaching that build on these experiences and students' prior knowledge.

Beginning teachers should be prepared to find out more about communities, families, and individual students. As teachers become aware of family and community values, norms, and experiences, they can help mediate the "boundary crossing" that many students must manage between home and school, and they can better engage their students' parents in the work of the school.

Teachers should know how to examine their own cultural assumptions to understand how these shape their starting points for practice, while also knowing how to uncover students' strengths, interests, and ways of communicating and behaving. To instruct students who learn in different ways, teachers need a repertoire of teaching strategies that respond to different learning styles and approaches. They need to diagnose *how* students learn as well as what they know by using a wide range of formal and informal assessment tools that are appropriate for students of different cultural and language backgrounds. They should know as well about curriculum content and materials that are inclusive of the contributions and perspectives of different groups.

In addition to the wide range of languages and cultures in most classrooms, another kind of diversity is the range of learning differences among students, including special education needs increasingly common in most classrooms. In teaching students with exceptional needs, teachers must understand differences in how people learn and process information, including the nature of common learning disabilities, such as dyslexia, developmental delays, autism, and attention deficit disorder. Teachers should be aware that many conditions can be very mild (hardly recognizable) to very severe. For common disabilities (for example, auditory or visual processing problems), teachers should have a basic repertoire of assessments, strategies, and adaptations that can help students gain access to the material they are teaching. At a minimum, teachers should understand how they can make appropriate adaptations for special needs students around time, the size or difficulty of tasks, the kinds of assistance offered (including technological supports), the way input is offered (auditory, visual, and so forth), and the kind of output required (how students demonstrate their learning). For the many students who have reading disabilities, teachers should have a working knowledge of strategies for supporting basic instruction and routine accommodations.

In addition, beginning teachers should have some understanding of the special education eligibility and placement process and how to work with other professionals and parents within these processes.

They need to know where to find additional information about specific diagnoses, disabilities, and services. And beginning teachers should know how to contribute to and implement individualized education plans (IEPs) for students in their classrooms. In short, teachers should be able to teach responsively, based on close study of their students' learning and an understanding of how to support learning differences.

Assessing Student Learning

If the central task of teaching is enabling learners with very different experiences, learning styles, and starting points to acquire common, high-level knowledge and skills, teachers must have many tools for tapping into what students think and be able to adapt instruction to their needs. Assessment of student learning is an integral part of the learning process. A generation ago, it was considered sufficient if teachers knew how to give tests that matched learning objectives. Today we know that assessment used to discover what students understand and how they are reasoning about a subject area can be a powerful tool in targeting instruction so as to move learning forward. Teaching, learning, and assessment must be understood as interactive and cyclical; for example, assessments of student learning should help improve teaching and subsequent learning. This is very different from thinking of these three as discrete, linear activities.

Beginning teachers must be knowledgeable about formative assessment that is carried out *during* the instructional process for the purpose of improving teaching or learning. They must be skillful in using various assessment strategies and tools such as observation, student conferences and interviews, written work, and discussions, as well as responses on tests and performance tasks. They must be knowledgeable about formative assessment that is carried out during the instructional process for the purpose of improving teaching or learning. Such assessments should be infused throughout the instructional process to help make students' thinking visible as they progress through a course of study, enable feedback about their work that guides revisions in their thinking and performance, and plan teaching so that it is responsive to what students need to know and how they learn.

Knowing how to give feedback that is concrete and productive is a key skill for teachers, along with knowing how to help students learn to self-assess. Teachers must not merely give feedback about whether answers are right or wrong; they must link feedback explicitly to clear performance standards and provide students with strategies for improvement and opportunities for revision. Teachers should understand the importance of providing feedback throughout the learning process, rather than only at the end, as well as the importance of offering positive feedback that identifies strengths along with constructive feedback that focuses on a limited number of key points that can be addressed in revisions.

Most important, teachers must be able to use insights from assessment to plan and revise instruction, using assessment information to inform moment-to-moment decisions in the classroom (for example, whether students need more explanation of a new concept), short-term planning (for example, the design of upcoming lessons), and long-term planning (for example, the development of larger units of study). In order to do this well, teachers must be able to assess students' prior knowledge, so that they can determine where to begin instruction, and they should have a working idea of typical learning progressions within subject matter domains, so that they know what they are helping students toward and how to back up if students do not immediately understand. At the individual and group level, teachers should be able to use data from different kinds of assessments to evaluate patterns of student strengths and weaknesses so that they can build on student strengths and target instruction where it is needed.

In planning assessment, teachers must know how to choose or develop assignments that represent their goals for learning (for example, reading books and newspapers, conducting experiments, developing explanations), and they need to know how to align standards, assessments, and learning experiences so that students will be able to succeed on the assignments as a result of the activities they have undertaken.

Beginning teachers should know how to use data systematically to make judgments about the specific aspects of instructional strategies that may be hindering learning. They should be able to assess their own instruction and assessment and determine, for example, whether tasks they have chosen are appropriate given the instruction students have had, are appropriate for second-language learners or students with special needs, and whether they generate good information for both student and teacher learning.

Teachers also have responsibilities for giving grades and reporting to parents about student progress. They need to know how to construct appropriate and informative summative assessments that are carried out primarily for the purpose of evaluating knowledge, giving grades, or certifying student proficiency. These assessments should afford students opportunities to demonstrate higher-level skills and provide multiple ways to demonstrate their proficiency, as well as evaluate students in relation to performance expectations. Teachers should understand principles of grading practices, including the kinds of information that grades should convey and the benefits and limitations of different kinds of grading systems.

Beginning teachers should understand the kinds of standardized tests that are used in national, state, and district-level assessments. This includes an understanding of what different tests measure, what can and cannot be inferred about student understanding from scores on a given test, and how to interpret the scores for improving instruction and informing parents about their children's achievements. Teachers also should know about the beneficial and harmful effects of different uses of high-stakes assessments. With this knowledge, teachers can design their curriculum and instruction to maximize the benefits of the information that tests provide and minimize potential harmful effects of high-stakes tests that can occur if the curriculum is narrowed or data are used to make inappropriate placement decisions.

Managing the Classroom

Many beginning teachers, especially those who are underprepared, focus much of their concern on classroom management, especially as it pertains to student discipline. Organizing a classroom for learning is extremely important to safeguard valuable time and to create a positive environment for teaching and learning. However, effective classroom management extends far beyond rules for classroom conduct and procedures to deal with misbehavior. Teachers who know how to structure activities and interactions so that they are orderly, purposeful, and based on common understandings of what to do and how to behave give students more opportunity to succeed because they understand what is expected of them. Given a strong curriculum, well-developed sense of community, and clear routines that have been established, teachers will encounter less problematic behavior by students.

To establish a well-functioning classroom in which learning occurs, beginning teachers first need to know how to create meaningful instruction that is motivating and engaging. The most fundamental elements in supporting student learning and engagement are choosing tasks that are developmentally appropriate and intrinsically interesting and providing supports that help students succeed.

Second, beginning teachers must know how to develop a learning environment within the classroom that supports a sense of belonging and commitment to the welfare of the group, as well as a sense of responsibility to cooperate with and help one another academically and socially. In order to develop such a community, teachers need to know how to help students learn to interact with one another respectfully (something that many students need to be taught), how to design cooperative learning activities in which focused learning occurs for all of the students, and how to work with parents to extend a working partnership into the home.

Third, beginning teachers must know how to organize the classroom to provide an orderly, purposeful environment that optimizes learning time and minimizes distractions. This includes knowing how to maintain the flow of activities; being alert to student responses and adapting instruction as needed to maintain attention, clear up misunderstandings, or attend to problems; and working with students to establish well-understood norms of behavior. It also includes knowing how to set up productive routines and procedures with respect to the physical setting of the room, transitions into and out of the room, roles and expectations during group work and independent work, general tasks such as distributing materials, tasks specific to particular classroom routines such as taking attendance or moving student desks, and engagement in specific instructional activities such as how to participate in discussions.

Fourth, beginning teachers should know how to repair and restore student behavior in the relatively rare circumstances in which students are disruptive or disrespectful. When a student behaves in ways that are counterproductive to the classroom goals and norms, teachers should know that there are many strategies to choose from and should be able to evaluate the student's particular learning situation and needs, the history of the student's behaviors, the context of the class, and the severity of the problem in light of classroom and school policy. Beginning teachers should know how to use unobtrusive methods of regaining students' attention in cases of minor disruption, and how to use conflict resolution skills in cases of clashes between students. They should know how to evaluate specific classroom management programs and how to explicitly model and teach desired behavior, including reasoning skills that help students begin to evaluate their own behavior, modify their actions, and find solutions to problems so that long-term improvements in interactions occur.

In Sum . . .

There is much that beginning teachers need to know before they take on responsibility for a classroom. In particular, they must take responsibility for teaching all children. In order to fulfill this enormous responsibility, they must

- Know their subject well and know how to teach it to students
- Understand how children learn and develop
- Be able to observe, monitor, and assess children to gain accurate feedback about their learning and development

- Know themselves—understand their own language and culture and know how to learn about other cultures with different language patterns and ways of knowing
- Be able to develop a curriculum and learning activities that connect what they know about their students to what the students need to learn
- Know how to teach specific subject matter in ways that are accessible, anticipating and addressing student conceptions and misconceptions
- Know how to develop and use assessments that measure learning standards and how to use the results to plan teaching that will address student learning needs
- Know how to use systematic inquiry, including how to observe an individual child in interaction with different tasks and other students to diagnose his or her needs
- Be able to evaluate why children may be responding or behaving in particular ways given the context of the classroom, the individual nature of the learning challenges, and the child's life outside school
- Be able to develop interventions, track changes, and revise their instructional strategies as necessary

---

What Do Teachers Need to Know? Quick Summary

- Teachers need to know how students *learn and develop* and how they *acquire and use language*.
- Teachers need to understand their *subject matter* and the *purposes of curriculum*.
- Teachers need to know and understand *teaching:* how to *teach subject matter* so it can be understood by diverse learners, how to *assess learning,* and how to *manage a classroom effectively*.

Chapter Two

How Can Teachers Acquire the Knowledge They Need?

Although knowledge about teaching and learning has grown, the odds that teachers will have access to this knowledge are far less than certain. This is both because of wide variations in the nature and quality of teacher education programs and the fact that a substantial number of individuals enter teaching without completing any teacher education. The majority of individuals enter teaching in the traditional fashion with formal preparation from an undergraduate or graduate teacher education program, but more and more new teachers come through alternative pathways where the rigor of the preparation ranges from excellent to nearly nonexistent. And in recent years, an increasing number of teachers have been hired on emergency permits or waivers without having experienced any formal preparation. Today, more than 15 percent of beginning teachers enter teaching through nontraditional pathways. Whether traditional or not, the kind and quality of preparation teachers receive can vary widely.

Prospective teachers also vary greatly in their knowledge and skills before they enter preparation. Some come steeped in their content area but unfamiliar with children, curriculum, and schools. Others, though knowledgeable about child development, are ignorant about particular areas of content or instruction or classroom management. Still others have years of working with children or young adults in settings outside of schools—Sunday school, youth groups, and the like. Many are well educated and have the "book" knowledge relevant to teaching and learning but lack the skills and experiences necessary to transform that knowledge into effective practice. Some have a good sense of how to present information to students who learn easily in the way they teach, but they lack the skills to reach students who learn in different ways, have gaps in their knowledge, or have particular learning difficulties.

How can we create programs and learning environments that ensure this diverse teacher candidate pool will develop the knowledge, skills, and dispositions that allow them to be successful in the classroom with all the children they serve? What knowledge and skills are prerequisite to entering the classroom? What aspects of learning to teach can be acquired on the job if beginning teachers' experiences are properly structured?

Clearly a range of undergraduate and postbaccalaureate programs that respond to the knowledge and experiences brought by different kinds of recruits is needed. No single approach will meet the needs of all prospective teachers optimally. However, all must ensure that candidates understand the basics of learning, development, curriculum, and teaching before they are asked to practice independently. Where prospective teachers are learning on the job—whether through student teaching or internships—they should be supervised by expert veterans who are available daily to coach, model, and oversee decisions in the areas of curriculum development, instruction, and the needs of individual students. How to structure this supervision so that it provides adequate expertise and oversight is one of the key program issues needing attention in both traditional and nontraditional settings. How to teach the content that is needed in a way that enables teachers to *use* the knowledge they have acquired is another.

These problems are not unique to teaching. Indeed, they affect all professional education. The curriculum for teacher education should be shaped both by what teachers need to learn and by how they learn. This means, first of all, that the content should be organized so that teachers gain a mental map of what is involved in effective teaching and what factors influence student learning. The domains outlined in this volume provide the elements of such a map and create a foundation on which teachers can continue to build. With this schema for their work and learning, teachers can seek out and add knowledge about specific techniques throughout their careers.

Structuring teacher education in terms of *how* teachers learn requires organizing the curriculum in a scope and sequence that capitalizes on teacher development—moving from a focus on self to a focus on student learning and from the foundations of learning theories to their implications for teaching. It also means finding ways for teachers to learn about practice *in* practice, so that concrete applications can be made and problems of practice can be raised, analyzed, and addressed. Thus, beginning teachers need consistent opportunities to apply what they are learning, analyze what happens, and adjust their efforts accordingly. They need to engage in inquiry and reflection about learning, teaching, and curriculum, as well as direct instruction in specific areas of content. All teachers, regardless of their route into the classroom, need these opportunities before they first become the sole teacher of record.

Central to the design of a teacher education curriculum—whether traditional or alternative—is the fact that teachers need both to acquire a set of skills and they need to become "adaptive experts." This means they must become able both to use efficient routines and to seek out and apply new strategies in situations where routines are not enough. Since teacher education cannot impart a body of knowledge that comprises everything a teacher will ever need to know, it must lay a foundation for lifelong learning. Given the relatively short time available for preparing teachers in both traditional and alternative programs and the fact that not everything can be taught, teacher preparation should be designed to help teachers learn from their practice and from the insights of others when they assume their initial teaching responsibilities.

How Teachers Develop and Learn

To design successful teacher education, it is important to understand how teachers' practice develops. For example, most teachers focus initially on themselves—what others think about them as teachers and their ability to control the classroom—and then eventually on students and their learning. Some teachers take a long time to move from a focus on self to a focus on students. And there are some teachers who never reach the stage of attending to student learning—who do not feel compelled to adjust their teaching if students do not learn and who do not know what might be done if some students are having difficulty. Teacher education can influence whether—and how quickly—teachers move from concern about themselves to concern for their students and a set of problem-solving strategies to promote student success. Strategies that involve teachers in analyzing learning and relating it to teaching are particularly useful in helping beginning teachers focus on learning and how to support it.

Teachers also progress from "novice" to more "expert" thinking about teaching—growing more able to deal with the many aspects of classroom life and to attend to the intellectual work of students. Experts in teaching—like experts in other fields—can quickly analyze complex situations and bring to bear many sources of knowledge about how to respond to them. They also have a broader and more flexible repertoire of skills they can use to achieve their goals. Teacher education that develops teachers' abilities to analyze teaching and expands their repertoire of teaching strategies—along with knowledge of when different strategies are likely to be useful—helps beginners move more quickly toward expertise.

Teachers also develop dispositions about what it means to be a teacher. Chief among these is the disposition to continue to seek strategies for reaching students who are not initially successful. Being a professional involves not simply "knowing the answers" but also having the skills and the will to evaluate one's practice and search for new answers when needed, both at the classroom level and the school level. Teacher education that helps teachers diagnose what is going on in problematic situations—when students are not learning, for example—and seek out other resources or knowledge to address the problem help develop this crucial disposition.

Problems of Learning to Teach

To develop beginning teachers who will become skilled practitioners who continue to learn, it is necessary to address three common problems associated with learning to teach: misconceptions about teaching, the problem of enactment, and the problem of complexity.

Misconceptions About Teaching

Learning to teach requires that new teachers come to understand teaching in ways quite different from what they have learned from their experience as students. These earlier experiences as students create strong preconceptions about teaching and learning that new teachers bring with them to the profession.[1]

Prospective teachers tend to start with views of teaching that focus more on the teacher's personality and less on the role of subject matter or pedagogical knowledge. They often believe that teaching is merely transmitting information and enthusiastically encouraging students, rather than assessing student learning to guide purposefully organized learning experiences with carefully staged supports. They also often underestimate the importance of the home and community contexts in teaching. If preconceptions about teaching are not addressed, prospective teachers can unconsciously cling to ineffective practices and fail to learn more beneficial approaches.

Programs that successfully change beginning teachers' understandings about teaching and learning use their students' initial beliefs about teaching as a springboard for surfacing and confronting misconceptions. They use structured discussions and guided observations of classrooms as means for candidates to share their initial views about teaching so these can be addressed. These instructional strategies provide opportunities for candidates to examine, analyze, and develop a vision of teaching that leads to higher achievement for diverse learners.

The Problem of Enactment

Helping teachers learn to teach effectively requires that they not only learn to "think like a teacher" but also that they be able to put what they know into action—what has been called "*the problem of enactment*."[2] Teachers must be able to *do* a wide variety of things, many of them simultaneously. Meeting this challenge requires much more than simply knowing one's subject matter or discussing ideas about teaching.

The issues teachers face regarding enactment are similar to those encountered in other professional fields but are even more challenging. For example, teachers do many more things at once, with many more clients assembled at one time, than do most other professionals. Developing an authoritative classroom presence, good radar for watching what many different students are doing and feeling at each moment, and skills for explaining, questioning, discussing, giving feedback, constructing tasks, facilitating work, and managing the classroom—all at once—is not simple.

If the information needed to teach well emerges during the practice itself, then teacher candidates need to have opportunities to practice and reflect on teaching early on and continuously in their preparation and during their initial entry to teaching. When well-supervised practicum and student-teaching experiences precede or are conducted jointly with course work, studies find that students are better able to connect theoretical learning to practice, more comfortable and confident in learning to teach, and more able to enact what they are learning in ways that are effective for students.[3]

Experience alone does not accomplish these goals. Seeing practices modeled and analyzing how, when, and why they work is key. Teachers who learn to teach without guidance often learn merely to cope rather than promote learning for all their students, and they can acquire bad habits that are hard to unlearn. Researchers have found that the process of learning to enact new skills is best supported by skilled coaching in peer support groups that allow teachers to develop, strengthen, and refine teaching skills together. Teachers hone their skills when they go through a process of learning, experimenting, and reflecting on their practice with feedback from peers and more expert practitioners. This, in turn, strengthens their ability both to implement new approaches and to fine-tune their efforts to produce student achievement gains. Such supports are characteristic of high-quality alternative route programs as well as high-quality college and university-based programs that are more traditionally organized.

The Problem of Complexity

Teachers typically work with many students at once and have to juggle many academic and social goals requiring trade-offs from moment to moment and day to day. As McDonald explains, "real teaching happens within a wild triangle of relations—among teacher, students, subject—and the points of this triangle shift continuously. What shall I teach amid all that I should teach? How can I grasp it myself so that my grasping might enable theirs? What are they thinking and feeling—toward me, toward each other, toward the thing I am trying to teach? How near should I come, how far off should I stay? How much clutch, how much gas?"[4]

Although some aspects of teaching can be made somewhat routine, they still will be influenced by changing student needs and unexpected classroom events. And many other decisions in teaching cannot be made routine because they are contingent upon student responses and the particular objectives sought at a given moment. Helping beginning teachers learn to think systematically about this complexity is extremely important.

Some teacher education approaches do not adequately respond to these problems. For example, telling teachers in general ways about strategies that might be used in the classroom, without examples and models, does not typically lead to deep understanding or enactment. Developing routines can be helpful and can free up teachers' attention for other aspects of their work; however, offering only routines does not help teachers develop the diagnostic and instructional skills for dealing with students who require different approaches or additional supports if they are to learn successfully. Because teachers have multiple goals, students are many and diverse, and teaching requires that many different areas of knowledge be integrated, teachers must learn to analyze what is going on in the classroom and make sound decisions about curriculum, instruction, assessment, and classroom management in the light of the particular students they teach.

How Can Teachers Acquire the Knowledge They Need? Quick Summary

- The teacher education curriculum should be shaped by what teachers need to learn—as outlined in this volume—and by how they learn through a developmental process of study, reflection, and application.

- Programs should address the key problems of learning to teach—dispelling the simplistic notions and misconceptions acquired as a K–12 student, helping teachers enact theory in practice, and helping them deal with the complexities of teaching by learning to *analyze* teaching and learning.

- Because teachers must learn *about* practice *in* practice, all programs—both traditional and alternative—should ensure well-supervised practicum opportunities, closely connected to course work, where they can learn from expert veterans who can model and coach effective teaching.

- Programs should help teachers develop a broad repertoire of teaching strategies and an understanding of when to use them to meet different purposes and needs.

- Programs should help teachers become *adaptive experts* who can both use efficient routines and develop new strategies when routines are not enough.

Chapter Three

Implications for Teacher Preparation

In the recent past, traditional teacher preparation often has been criticized for being overly theoretical, having little connection to practice, offering fragmented and incoherent courses, and lacking in a clear, shared conception of teaching among faculty. Programs that are largely a collection of unrelated courses and that lack a common conception of teaching and learning have been found to be feeble agents for affecting practice among new teachers. This can also be the case in some alternative routes that give short shrift to critical content of teacher education, keeping course work separate from unguided practice that provides little meaningful support to beginning candidates.

Beginning in the late 1980s, teacher education reforms began to produce program designs representing more integrated, coherent programs that emphasize a consistent vision of good teaching. These programs—which included postbaccalaureate alternative models as well as traditional programs—created stronger links between subject matter and pedagogical courses and connected clinical experiences to formal coursework, in part by interweaving student teaching with coursework and by infusing classroom practices into the curriculum. The programs teach teachers to do more than simply implement particular techniques; they help teachers learn to think pedagogically, reason through dilemmas, investigate problems, and analyze student learning to develop appropriate curriculum for a diverse group of learners. Studies have found that such programs have a greater impact on the initial conceptions, practices, and effectiveness of new teachers than others that are less coherent and less intent on connecting theory and practice.

Some programs have graduates that report significantly greater feelings of preparedness than their peers and are more highly rated by employers, who say they seek out these candidates because they are more effective in the classroom from their very first days of teaching. Such programs have a number of common features, including

- A common core curriculum grounded in knowledge of development, learning, subject matter pedagogy, and assessment, taught in the context of practice

- Well-defined standards of practice and performance used to guide the design and assessment of coursework and clinical work

- Extended clinical experiences (at least thirty weeks) that are interwoven with coursework and are carefully mentored

- Strong relationships between universities and schools that share standards of good teaching which are consistent across courses and clinical work

- Use of case study methods, teacher research, performance assessments, and portfolio examinations that relate teachers' learning to classroom practice[1]

Strong alternative route programs that generate confident beginning teachers who help students learn share many of these same characteristics. Research indicates that the most successful alternative programs

- Have high entry-level standards

- Give solid pedagogical training in subject-matter instruction, management, curriculum, and working with diverse students

- Afford intensive mentoring and supervision from carefully chosen, well-trained staff

- Expose candidates to excellent teaching and modeling of good practice

- Develop strong relationships among the partners

- Provide plenty of guided practice in lesson planning and teaching prior to a candidate taking on full responsibility as the teacher of record
- Have high exit standards[2]

What these programs do is consistent with research that indicates that new teachers learn best in a community that enables them to develop a *vision* for their practice; *knowledge* about teaching, learning, and children; *dispositions* about how to use this knowledge; *practices* that allow them to act on their intentions and beliefs; and *tools* that support their efforts. This framework for learning to teach is shown in Figure 3.1. It is not surprising that it mirrors the knowledge and skills teachers need to be successful with all students, illustrated earlier in Figure 1.1.

A curricular *vision* involves teachers' sense of where they are going and how they are going to get students there. Images of good practice from clinical practice, videotapes, and studies of excellent practitioners can help new teachers reflect on their work, guide their practice, and direct their future learning. Such visions connect important values and goals to concrete classroom practices and provide a basis for teachers to develop and assess their teaching and their students' learning.

Teachers' *knowledge* of their subject and how to make it accessible to others relies on an understanding of both the content and the learning process. Teachers need to possess a rich, coherent conceptual map of the discipline, an understanding of how knowledge is developed and validated within different social contexts, an understanding of why the subject is important, and an understanding of how to communicate knowledge of that subject to others. This, in turn, requires an understanding of learners and their development.

To put what they know into practice, teachers also need to develop *tools* for use in the classroom. *Conceptual tools* include learning theories and ideas about teaching (concepts such as the zone of proximal development or culturally relevant teaching), while *practical* tools include textbooks, assessment tools, curriculum guides, and other instructional materials. Such tools help teachers work smarter.

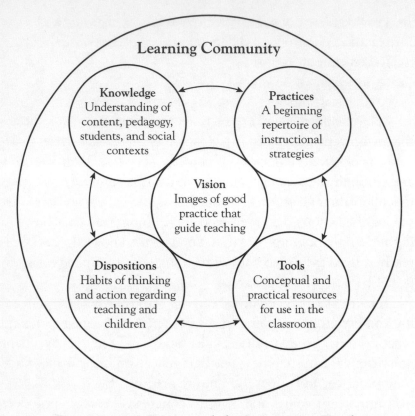

Figure 3.1. A Framework for Learning to Teach.

These understandings and tools need to be integrated into a set of *practices* for use in the classroom. The practices can include instructional activities such as explaining concepts, holding discussions, designing experiments, developing simulations, planning debates, or organizing writing workshops. Practices also include activities such as designing and carrying out unit plans and daily lessons, developing assessments, and offering feedback that is constructive and specific. Beginning teachers should learn not only the content of these strategies but also when, where, how and why to use particular approaches.

In addition to knowledge that is connected to tools and practices, teachers need to develop a set of *dispositions*—or habits of thinking and action—about teaching, children, and the role of the teacher. These include the disposition to reflect and learn from practice, a willingness to take responsibility for children's learning, determination and persistence in working with children until they succeed, and the will to continue to seek new approaches to teaching that will allow greater success with students.

Finally, learning to teach occurs most productively within professional *communities*, such as experienced colleagues who work with cohorts of student teachers. Groups of educators who share norms and practices can be especially powerful influences on learning, especially when there are collective knowledge and common goals across fieldwork and courses. This means that teacher education programs—whether traditional or alternative—need to develop strong partnerships with schools in which veterans and teachers-in-training share standards of practice and work collaboratively to put them into action.

In sum, contemporary research suggests that learning about teaching best develops when prospective teachers encounter content in contexts in which it can be applied. Teachers benefit from participating in the culture of teaching by working with the *materials and tools of teaching practice* and by examining teaching plans and student learning while immersed in theory about learning, development, and subject matter. They also benefit from *participating in practice* as they observe teaching, work closely with experienced teachers, and work with students to use what they are learning. And this learning is strengthened when it is embedded within a broad *community of practitioners*—experienced faculty, other student teachers, and other educators.

Promising Pedagogies

Although research on the pedagogies of teacher education is still in the early stages of development, researchers have assembled evidence about particular practices that help teachers develop the kinds of teaching expertise necessary to assure that all children learn. In addition to the usual tools of education—carefully chosen readings and materials, well-crafted lectures, and descriptions or demonstrations of particular strategies—a number of pedagogies have emerged in response to the perennial problems of learning to teach. Many have been developed explicitly to aid in the professional problem of helping novices connect theory to practice by focusing upon learning *in* practice through both direct instruction and inquiry.

Cognitive psychologists have found that "deliberate practice"—purposefully rehearsing certain kinds of performances—is particularly important to the development of expertise. Effective teacher education programs provide structured opportunities to practice particular strategies and use specific tools in the classroom setting. In addition, teacher educators in effective programs use examples of student work, artifacts from the classroom, videotapes of teaching and learning, and cases of teaching to help teachers relate their coursework to real problems of practice in classrooms.

None of these pedagogies is a silver bullet. Each has particular strengths and limitations, all can be implemented well or poorly, but in combination these strategies have the potential to greatly enhance the learning of new teachers.

Student Teaching and Internships

Perhaps the most pervasive pedagogy in teacher education is that of supervised student teaching, which has long been acknowledged as having a profound impact on teachers' learning. Some clinical training experiences are also called internships, usually denoting that the teacher-in-training takes on more direct teaching responsibility but continues to practice with instruction under close supervision. But the student teaching or internship experience varies dramatically both within and across programs, depending on how cooperating teachers are recruited and what the expectations are for both the novice and cooperating teacher. The length varies from less than eight weeks to more than thirty weeks, the extent and quality of modeling and guidance from minimal to extensive, the clarity regarding practices desired from obscure to well-defined. The mentoring also varies widely, with some novice teachers practicing under daily supervision that includes planning, coaching, modeling, and demonstration, and others never having the chance to see modeled what they are trying to create in practice.

Different strategies for student teaching bring with them different benefits and limitations. For example, having multiple settings for practice teaching may allow student teachers to consider how contexts make a difference in the choice of strategies and how to use them. At the same time, multiple short placements reduce the opportunities to deeply understand a group of students and a kind of practice, and may make it difficult for student teachers to learn how what came before influences what is happening now in the classroom. Shorter placements also place burdens on schools without the compensating benefits of the contribution a more seasoned student teacher (for example, one who spends an entire semester or year) can make, thus sometimes making it more difficult to maintain strong partnerships for practicum placements. There is no one right answer to these trade-offs. What is important is that prospective teachers' clinical experiences are constructed with careful consideration of *what* the experience should be like and *how* it will be connected to the curriculum, so that the program can optimize the experiences offered.

Successful clinical training experiences have the following characteristics:

- Clarity of goals, including the use of standards guiding the performances and practices to be developed
- Modeling of good practices by more expert teachers in which teachers make their thinking visible
- Frequent opportunities for practice with continuous formative feedback and coaching
- Multiple opportunities to relate classroom work to university coursework
- Graduated responsibility for all aspects of classroom teaching
- Structured opportunities to reflect on practice with an eye toward improving it

The support offered during initial clinical work is critical in enabling beginning teachers to make sense of their experience and learn from it. Studies suggest that powerful learning does not usually occur from letting a teacher "sink or swim." Expert guidance and peer support are important for novices if they are to receive the modeling, coaching, and feedback they need. Program designs that include more early practicum experiences and longer student teaching integrated with coursework—especially where the vision of teaching in the placement aligns with the practices being taught in courses—have been found to make a difference in teachers' practices, confidence, effectiveness, and long-term commitment to teaching.

Settings that foster more powerful clinical learning feature teams of teachers who work together, using state-of-the-art practices based on sound research, collaboratively developing curriculum and instruction, engaging in peer review of each other's practice, and conducting ongoing inquiry into the effectiveness of the approaches they use. Some school districts and universities have jointly created such settings in high-quality alternative route programs where candidates learn to teach in high-performing schools through a careful transition from assisting and practice teaching in the classroom of an expert veteran to increasingly independent teaching under the direction of a skilled mentor or team of colleagues who support lesson planning, provide coaching, and are available to address problems that arise.[3]

Other school-university partnerships have created sites such as professional development schools for the training of preservice teachers and the continued development of expert veteran teachers. Where they are well-implemented, these professional development schools function like teaching hospitals in medicine, which improve professionwide practice through research, development, and training. Studies of highly developed professional development schools have found that teachers who have done long-term student teaching in such programs feel more knowledgeable and prepared to teach and are viewed by supervisors as better prepared than other new teachers. Veteran teachers working in these schools report improvements in curriculum and teaching as a result of the professional development, research, and mentoring that are part of the effort, and some studies have documented gains in areas of student achievement directly tied to interventions the schools have undertaken with their university partners.[4]

Teaching Portfolios and Performance Tasks

Although clinical experiences provide the opportunity for practice, they are often rather haphazard opportunities that may not ensure the occasion to encounter certain kinds of teaching problems or develop and demonstrate particular skills. More structured performance tasks can be used to provide opportunities for student teachers to demonstrate certain practices and analyze them, along with their effects.

Some teacher education programs have developed specific performance tasks they require of candidates (for example, planning and conducting a lesson, delivering a lecture, managing a discussion, completing and teaching a curriculum unit) around which they organize coursework and assessment. In some cases, these tasks are presented, evaluated, and repeated until they reach a standard of competent performance. In addition, assessments for teacher licensing and advanced certification have begun to incorporate performance elements that require teachers to demonstrate their proficiency on specific tasks teachers must engage in in the classroom.

These assessments are generally part of a larger teaching portfolio—a collection of materials from the teacher's work, such as lesson plans, assignments, samples of student work, and videotapes of the teacher in action. Portfolios are used in many preservice programs and some high-quality alternative route programs as part of the process for candidates to document their mastery of the standards of teaching practice necessary for entry into the profession. As teaching tools, portfolios can provide opportunities for candidates to closely examine and analyze the process and outcomes of teaching and learning. The use of authentic classroom materials enables student teachers and teacher educators jointly to examine and analyze a "common text" to which all have access. The conception of a common text is a key idea that unites analyses of videotapes of teaching, analyses of student work samples, and analyses of portfolio or performance assessment entries. Typically, teacher educators engage students in examining both texts produced by *other* teachers and their *own* materials, thus producing a dialogue and multiple points of feedback about their evolving practice as new teachers. Common texts also serve to develop a common language regarding the attributes of good teaching and serious learning.

Some portfolios used to assess the competence of beginning teachers involve student teachers in designing a unit, teaching a set of lessons within the unit, developing an assessment plan, analyzing work samples from students, reflecting on their teaching outcomes, and revising their plans. Evidence suggests that teachers learn a great deal from completing and scoring such portfolios, in part because they focus teachers' reflection on content-specific professional standards that are used for evaluating the portfolio. Teaching practices that are reviewed, revised, and discussed in light of shared standards about teaching and learning help ground and focus the work. Furthermore, the standards serve as public criteria by which performances can be measured.

Researchers have found that portfolios organized around specific standards can support teachers' development of a conceptual framework about teaching, link theoretical learning to classroom practice, and help teachers analyze and refine their practices by providing structured opportunities for them to document and describe their teaching and their learning and to reflect upon what, how, and why they teach.

Analyses of Teaching and Learning

Learning in and from practice is accomplished not only by placing student teachers in classrooms. It can also happen through strategic documentation of practice by using plans, videotapes, and work samples from the classroom that can be systematically studied by groups of teachers who conduct a focused analysis of particular ideas or practices.

In addition to the examinations of teaching and learning that are encouraged in portfolios, some scholars of teaching have developed videotape and multimedia tools for close study of the work of expert teachers. These include extensive videotapes of mathematics teaching and associated artifacts of student work and teacher plans mounted in a hypermedia platform by Deborah Ball and colleagues at the University of Michigan; the Carnegie Foundation's Knowledge Media Lab that documents the teaching practice of accomplished teachers through Web-based collections of materials organized around their classroom strategies and inquiries; and the videotapes and analyses of teaching developed by James Stigler and Harold Stevenson as part of the Third International Mathematics and Science Study. Such efforts to document teaching have produced rich materials that can now be accessed by teacher educators for joint viewing, reviewing, and analysis by students.

Analyzing teaching artifacts in these ways has at least three advantages:

- It provides an opportunity for new teachers to think about the complexity of the classroom by studying the work of expert veterans who have shared their practice and their reasoning, as well as evidence of their students' achievement.

- It can help new teachers and teacher educators develop a shared understanding and common language about teaching.

- It enables new teachers time for reflection and reviewing (which is impossible in real-time observations of the classroom) while still using the real materials of practice.

Also important, such materials can support the analysis of learning and reinforce the teaching-learning connection. Using student work samples and other evidence of performance (videotapes of students working through problems, aggregated data about test performance), analyses of learning can focus on numerous issues that arise in the teaching and learning process, from challenges of student engagement, student understanding, and assessment to questions about how to frame the subject matter curriculum. Research on the use of videotapes of teaching and learning suggests that when groups of teachers repeatedly analyze these kinds of materials, their analysis and conversation gradually shifts from a focus on the teacher and what she is doing to a focus on student thinking and learning and how to support it.

Case Methods

As in other professions, including law, medicine, and business, engaging prospective teachers in reading and writing cases can help candidates bridge the gap between theory and practice and develop skills of reflection and close analysis. Cases can allow for the exploration of dilemmas as they occur in real classrooms, creating a bridge between learning from particular contexts and from more generalized theory about teaching and learning.

Typically, cases are accounts of teaching and learning that pose dilemmas, provide careful descriptions of contexts, and share evidence or data about outcomes of classroom situations. In teacher education programs, student teachers can read and analyze cases, discerning and reasoning through dilemmas and proposing strategies to respond to problems. Students can also write cases, learning to represent their experiences and analyze them through the lens of theory so that they and others can learn from these examples. There are a number of perspectives that cases may take: some focus on subject matter, probing how teachers design instruction to help students master content; some focus on students, developing teachers' ability to observe and analyze evidence of learning and development; and still others focus on contexts or culture, helping prepare teachers to teach students from diverse backgrounds and communities.

Case studies of children, frequently used in courses on human development, engage teachers in collecting and analyzing data through interviews and observation in order to better understand student learning, developmental progress, special needs, and the influences of school, home, and community contexts. Case analyses of curriculum and teaching focus on the development of instruction and the dilemmas in teaching particular concepts or ideas in order to review the relationship between teachers' intentions and students' learning and how teaching has mediated the two. Dilemma cases are often used to illustrate long-time teaching challenges—such as moral dilemmas, interpersonal difficulties, or cultural differences—and to engage teachers in deliberating, problem solving, and analyzing these challenges.

Research has found that well-taught cases can help teachers develop reasoning skills and move toward more expert and student-focused thinking by looking more systematically at the different influences on learning and understanding how theory relates to specific practices and, in turn, outcomes. Not all uses of case methods result in these outcomes, however. As some researchers point out: "Without learning opportunities that develop insights, raise other perspectives into view, and create bridges between theory and practice, cases may add up to interesting but uninstructive teaching stories that reinforce idiosyncratic or uniformed views of teaching."[5]

Instruction that helps case readers and writers increase their understanding includes

- Connections between events in the classroom and discussions and readings about principles of teaching and learning
- Guidance regarding how to collect and analyze data about students' thinking and learning
- Specific, concrete feedback on candidates' interpretations of what influenced learning that calls attention to principles of development, learning theory, teaching strategies, student factors, and context variables, thus ensuring that research informs candidates' explanations of how learning occurs

Inquiry and Action Research

Preparing teachers to learn from teaching throughout their careers requires a set of tools that develop the skills and practices of systematic, purposeful inquiry and critical reflection. Many teacher educators develop these abilities by engaging student teachers in systematic research in their classrooms and schools. Such experiences can help teachers not only deal with the complexity of practice but also overcome some of the limitations of their preconceived notions about teaching.

The process of practitioner inquiry includes all aspects of a research or inquiry process:

- Identifying questions of compelling interest (these may focus upon specific issues of teaching and learning as well as broader issues of schooling and society)
- Pursuing those questions through the collection of data (which may include observations of children, classroom or other observational field notes, interviews with children, parents, or other teachers, analysis of learning outcomes, or library research)
- Reflecting upon the questions through written work (journal entries, research memos) and discussion with peers, instructors, and master teachers

Practitioner research has been found to support teachers in developing the habits of reflection and analysis along with the important skills of data collection and observation. It can also help teachers learn how to watch students carefully and evaluate on a regular basis what seems to be working or not working in the classroom, while giving them the tools to test their hypotheses so that they can adjust their practice. Finally, these kinds of inquiries frequently inspire teachers to engage in additional learning as they encounter new arenas of knowledge through their research.

In Sum . . .

These pedagogies of teacher education—student teaching, performance assessments and portfolios, analyses of teaching and learning, case methods, and practitioner inquiry—are intended to support teachers' abilities to learn *in* and *from* practice. In different ways, each approach helps build the vision, knowledge, tools, practices, and dispositions of new teachers to reflect on and analyze their practice. The interrelationship among these pedagogies is also important. It is likely that these pedagogies work most powerfully as complements to one another—and some pedagogies (such as case study) may be particularly useful early on in programs whereas others (such as classroom research) may be best engaged once student teachers have had opportunities to critically examine their own experiences of schooling. It is important to note that these pedagogies can be used in the development of beginning teachers whether they come through traditional teacher education routes or alternative routes.

Of course, these approaches to teaching teachers are only as useful as the content they convey. Candidates cannot become competent and skillful by reflecting in the abstract. They need a solid body of knowledge to provide a foundation for the judgment and analytic ability they are developing. Assembling the appropriate content for teacher education in ways that make it vital, usable, and useful requires considering all the components of preparation in tandem: assuring that courses cohere and are sequenced to build on one another, critical concepts are taught not only by "mentioning" but by serious examination and repeated application, and that opportunities for clinical practice are tightly tied to the learning of important constructs. Teacher educators—whether they are university- or school-based—must construct integrated learning experiences, model the practices they want candidates to adopt, provide clear examples and standards that reflect what good teaching looks like and consists of, and help candidates hone their practice by carefully assessing candidates' learning and providing continuous intensive feedback. Expert teaching of teachers takes time, effort, and support—and its success depends on a supportive policy environment.

Implications for Teacher Preparation: Quick Summary

Effective traditional and alternative teacher education programs

- Offer a strong, carefully sequenced, coherent curriculum grounded in knowledge of learning, development, curriculum, teaching, and assessment

- Enable teachers to develop a *vision* for their practice linked to *knowledge* and *dispositions* about teaching, learning, and children, and enacted through concrete *tools* that allow them to implement their intentions and beliefs in the classroom

- Provide extended clinical practice under close supervision that is aligned and connected to learning of concepts and specific strategies and that allows graduated responsibility for the novice teacher

- Ensure tightly integrated learning in professional communities where effective practices are modeled, clear examples and standards are provided, and candidates are continually assessed, receiving intensive, ongoing feedback

- Use case methods, including video cases of teaching, analyses of teaching and learning, teacher inquiry, and performance assessments to relate learning to classroom practice

Chapter Four

Policy Recommendations

Today, despite what we know is needed to assure children qualified teachers, many states still allow such diversity of preparation—both in traditional academic and alternative routes to the classroom—and such weak standards of entry into the profession that thousands of individuals enter classrooms only to flail and fail and leave after a short time. Thousands of others enter, stay, and never master the knowledge and skill necessary to be minimally effective, let alone "highly qualified." Furthermore, once beginning teachers enter the classroom, they are all too often isolated from their more experienced veteran colleagues and left to "sink or swim" with no meaningful support to ensure that they develop into the highly qualified teachers that current policy rhetoric demands for all students.

At least 30 percent of new teachers leave the profession within the first five years of entry at great educational and financial cost to schools. Not only are teachers significantly more effective after their second year of teaching,[1] but such attrition is expensive. The costs of replacing beginners who leave average at least $8,000 per recruit,[2] dollars that could be more profitably spent on direct investments in classrooms. Research has confirmed that high rates of attrition from teaching are often a function of inadequate preparation and support in the early years, along with poor salaries and working conditions. New teachers who have had these supportive student teaching experiences and course work in such areas as learning theory and child development are more than twice as likely to stay in teaching as those who have missed these important elements of preparation.[3] And those who have been fortunate enough to experience strong mentoring and support in the first years of teaching also leave at much lower rates than those who are left to learn on their own.

To be sure, despite the wide range of problems that have historically beset teacher recruitment and preparation—difficulty recruiting the ablest students, underinvestment in teacher education programs, lack of coordination between colleges of teacher education and the arts and sciences faculty, and inadequate preservice time for prospective teachers to acquire the content knowledge, pedagogical knowledge, and clinical experiences they need to be successful in the classroom—universities and school districts have produced thousands of capable teachers. Nonetheless, access to good preparation, traditional or alternative, is haphazard at best. At worst, the current nonsystem results in far too many poorly prepared and unprepared teachers employed disproportionately in schools serving large numbers of low-income and "minority" students. These are the schools where the very best teachers are needed if we are in fact to "leave no child behind" and assure all children a chance for an excellent education that prepares them to compete in a global economy and participate in a democracy that relies on an educated citizenry.

As concerns about the quality of American education have been linked to evidence that teacher quality makes an important difference in outcomes, a variety of reforms to create more rigorous preparation, certification, and licensing have been launched. With these reforms, the quality of preparation appears to have noticeably improved in some places. But the outcomes of recent reforms are not straightforward. The plethora of policies has sometimes worked in contradictory ways. For example, individual state efforts to upgrade standards have resulted in more disparate test requirements and less reciprocity among states, which has made it harder for teachers trained in states where there are surpluses to teach in those where there are shortages. And the upgrading of standards for teacher education has in many states created a bimodal teaching force, with some candidates meeting higher standards but a growing number of others entering through backdoor routes, teaching on emergency permits when they do not pass the state tests or complete preparation requirements.

The same conditions pertained in medicine when Abraham Flexner published his landmark report on the state of medical education in the United States in 1910. Medical school programs at that time ranged in duration from three weeks to three years and were dramatically different in the scope and nature of knowledge they tapped. In his introduction to the report, Henry Pritchett, president of the Carnegie Foundation for the Advancement of Teaching, noted that although there was a growing science of medicine, most doctors did not get access to this knowledge because of the great unevenness in the medical training they received. He attributed this problem both to the fact that many doctors did not receive a formal education and to the failure of many universities to incorporate advances in medical education into their curricula. In the medical schools that had emerged in the previous decades, course work was frequently divorced from clinical work, and curriculum was often fragmented, superficial, and didactic—the same kinds of complaints that have dogged colleges of education since they took up the charge of educating teachers in the latter half of the twentieth century.

The eventual widespread reform of medical education occurred as the profession set standards for medical training—derived from research in the emerging sciences of medicine and the best practices of strong programs at that time—and infused these into the standards for accrediting professional programs and the standards for licensing and certifying medical candidates, who had to graduate from a professionally accredited program in order to sit for licensing and board certification examinations. Medical education was fashioned in large part on the curriculum developed at Johns Hopkins University, which included both course work in the sciences of medicine and clinical learning in the newly invented teaching hospital. Parallel processes of setting standards were later followed for law, engineering, nursing, psychology, accounting, architecture, and other occupations that became professions in the twentieth century.

In similar fashion, over the last two decades, the teaching profession has begun to codify the knowledge base for professional practice and to establish standards for the work of practitioners through the efforts of the National Board for Professional Teaching Standards, the more than thirty states comprising the Interstate New Teacher Assessment and Support Consortium (INTASC), and professional associations of educators and members of subject area disciplines. This work has been made possible by huge strides in our understanding of student learning and the teaching practices that support it. The standards developed by these bodies distinguish more effective from less effective practice, as demonstrated by several studies that have found, for example, that teachers who have met the standards and achieved National Board Certification produce stronger gains in student learning than teachers who have not met these standards.[4]

Nonetheless, in recent years, the policy debate surrounding teacher preparation has been very fractious, with one set of advocates insisting that there is little to teaching beyond knowing subject matter and calling for the deregulation of preparation and elimination of licensure. These opponents of preparation believe teachers need only a few "tricks of the trade" that can be picked up on the job. They also believe that thousands of talented individuals who want to enter the teaching force are kept out by trivial requirements whose sole purpose is to keep the "teacher education monopoly" in colleges and universities alive and well. In some policy environments, these views have resulted in the proliferation of weak alternative routes for entering the classroom, as well as the dilution of traditional preparation.

Another set of proponents has argued that better practice will result from professionalizing teaching, not by eliminating teacher preparation, and by creating more thoughtful policies regarding

- Accreditation of traditional and alternative preparation programs
- Licensing standards
- Recruitment and retention of beginning teachers, including supports for induction

In the past, a major stumbling block to meaningful accreditation and licensure reform has been a lack of consensus on the core curriculum necessary for teachers to master and the clinical experiences future teachers should encounter as they prepare for their teaching careers. This volume provides the basis for determining the necessary knowledge and skill development that a program—traditional or alternative—should offer if it is to be accredited, and presents the features of a core curriculum that can form the basis for a rigorous licensing system. It also describes policies that need to be in place to recruit, retain, and improve the practice of beginning teachers.

Development and Accreditation of Preparation Programs

As we noted earlier, prospective teachers are drawn from a variety of population pools and take a variety of pathways into the classroom. Although the vast majority—whether neophytes or career changers—still come through a teacher education program housed in a college or university, an increasing number enter teaching through alternative programs operated by districts or states. Some have considerable experience working with children; others have a great deal of experience as teachers of adults; still others come with deep knowledge of the subjects they wish to teach. Teacher preparation accreditation can accommodate this diversity by examining how every program assures that its graduates have the knowledge and skill described in the preceding chapters to be considered eligible for beginning to teach.

Depending on how the programs are structured and whom they recruit, programs will vary in emphasis on developing subject matter knowledge, pedagogical skills, and clinical supports. Nonetheless, taken together, any program should demonstrate how it ensures that its prospective teachers

- Know their subjects well and how to teach them to students
- Understand how children learn and develop

- Understand their own language and culture and know how to learn about other cultures
- Know how to develop a curriculum and learning activities that connect what they know about their students to what the students need to learn
- Know how to teach specific subject matter in ways that are accessible to a diverse range of students.
- Know how to develop and use assessments that measure learning standards and how to use the results to plan teaching that addresses student learning needs
- Know how to create and manage a respectful, purposeful classroom
- Are able to identify and plan for children's learning needs
- Are able to develop interventions, track changes, and revise their teaching strategies as necessary
- Are able to work with parents and their colleagues to create a common set of expectations and collective supports for students' learning

To be accredited, any program—traditional or alternative—should be able to demonstrate that, in combination, its selection criteria, the content of its courses, and the pedagogies it employs ensure that its teacher candidates have mastered the content and experiences identified in this report as necessary to producing effective beginning teachers. Programs that do not expose their candidates to this core curriculum and to rich, well-supervised clinical experiences should not be allowed to operate. In addition, accreditation should take into account the proportion of teachers trained by a program who enter and stay in teaching. Supporting programs whose selection and training process is unsuccessful in recruiting and retaining significant numbers of recruits in teaching is wasteful. It dilutes the overall quality of preparation accessible to candidates by spreading thin the limited dollars available for clinical training to cover individuals who are unlikely to make a career in teaching.

What policies can be developed to assure that this occurs?

• The federal government can carefully examine its processes of granting accreditation authority to organizations to assure that the organizations' accreditation processes determine that preparation programs, alternate or otherwise, are coherent; include the development of a vision of teaching that is responsive to student learning; and that provide, through candidate selection and training, the course work and the clinical experiences necessary to produce teachers who have mastered the knowledge and skills identified in this report.

• States can implement policies that take seriously the accreditation of *all* teacher education programs, traditional and alternative, and (1) close programs that do not meet rigorous accreditation criteria and (2) refuse to grant licenses to individuals who have not successfully completed accredited programs.

• States can implement data systems that track for all programs—traditional and alternative—their success in preparing candidates who demonstrate in performance assessments that they can teach and who enter and stay in teaching.

• Institutions that sponsor teacher education programs can evaluate their current programs against the curriculum recommendations proposed here and can take steps to strengthen the course work and clinical work they offer.

• States and institutions can ensure that reimbursement ratios and funding for professional education programs are comparable to what is provided for other clinically based professional programs, such as nursing and engineering.

In addition, policies can be developed to support the creation of high-quality programs in the communities where they are most needed. For example, just as the federal government has long sponsored efforts to improve the quality of medical education and the spread of teaching hospitals that are sites for high-quality training, it should sponsor efforts—with strong quality standards—for the development of high-quality teacher education programs, including strong links to professional development schools, where candidates can learn to teach in settings that are successful with diverse student populations in urban and poor rural communities that experience teacher shortages. These programs should meet three criteria: ensuring a high-quality teacher preparation experience, attracting local residents to the programs, and ensuring a pipeline from preparation to hiring.

This approach would merge the attributes of excellent preparation programs with the benefits of many alternate-route programs: the fact that they finance and prepare candidates explicitly for a given district; thus the district reaps the investment's benefits, and candidates know they will have a job. When there are high-quality programs with the components we have described here, the bargain is a good one. And some programs target local residents and longtime paraprofessionals already knowledgeable about and committed to their communities. Such opportunities could be encouraged by federal grants to urban universities and districts to create or expand programs that meet high standards for program quality and that support local candidates from preparation through hiring. An analog is the set of federal programs that have created programs specifically designed to prepare health professionals for urban communities and have established community health centers to support clinical preparation.[5]

Licensure Reform

Licensing is the legal means by which states establish the competence of members of professions, including teachers. It is meant to represent the minimum standard for responsible practice. In teaching, requirements for licensure typically include measures of basic skills and general academic ability, knowledge about teaching and learning, and subject matter knowledge, as well as some teaching experience. In many states, candidates for teaching must earn a minimum grade point average or achieve a minimum score on tests of basic skills, general academic ability, or general knowledge in order to be admitted to teacher education or gain a credential. In addition, they must take specific courses in education and complete a major or minor in the subject(s) to be taught or pass a subject matter test, or both.

Despite the many reforms of the past fifteen years, a number of states still do not require a coherent program of studies in the field to be taught, a core set of essential course work, or extended student teaching. Further, many states permit teachers to be hired without licenses or on emergency licenses without completing preparation or meeting other licensure requirements. Teacher licensure in the United States remains a patchwork of requirements, with little comparability across states and, in many states, no assurance that candidates who are allowed to teach have been exposed to, let alone mastered, the core curriculum and experiences this report has identified as necessary for a beginning teacher.

It is hard to imagine why the teaching knowledge needed to instruct first graders to read, write, and compute should vary from state to state, but vary it does. Licensing examinations for teachers differ as to content, quality, and extent of mastery that teachers must have in order to be qualified to enter the classroom. For example, during 2001–02, thirty-seven states required teaching candidates to pass tests of basic skills or general academic ability, thirty-three required them to pass tests of subject matter knowledge, and twenty-six required them to pass tests of pedagogical knowledge. Most of these tests were different from state to state and many candidates who left the state where they prepared to teach to take employment in another had to pass separate batteries of several tests in both states and take additional courses not required in the first state, at great expense of time and money. Many teachers who move between states leave the profession for other careers because of such obstacles.

The current hodgepodge of licensure exams poses three serious problems for those concerned about the quality of teachers entering the classroom:

1. Many of the tests being offered assess low-level or marginally relevant knowledge and skills, not the candidate's deep knowledge of subject matter and actual teaching skills.

2. Cut scores for these tests are sometimes low or are not enforced. When states have teaching shortages they often waive the testing requirement and allow hiring of those who have not passed the test.

3. The lack of consistency across states creates barriers to teacher mobility, which is a particular problem since many states have surpluses of teachers while others have shortages. The hiring of well-qualified teachers in all communities requires policies that can get teachers more effectively from where they are trained to where they are needed.

Whereas other professions control the content of licensure tests, teaching examinations are usually developed by testing companies or state agencies with little input from formal professional bodies. When it is solicited, input from practitioners is usually limited to reviewing test categories and items. Further, licensure tests have been criticized not only for lack of rigor but also for oversimplifying teaching and emphasizing classroom procedures over the complexities of instructional decision making.[6]

A major reason for the weakness of teacher licensing has been the absence of a consensus on a core curriculum upon which to build a rigorous test. This report provides the basis for the development of such a test—one that could be used by all states in much the same way that they currently use the multistate bar exam as one part of the licensure process to assure rigor and quality control across the country.

Such a test, like those used to certify doctors, lawyers, and architects, should demonstrate not only what teachers *know* about their subjects and how to teach them but also what they can *do* in the classroom; for example, whether they can plan and implement lessons to teach to standards, evaluate students' needs and design instruction to meet them, use a variety of effective teaching strategies, and maintain a purposeful, productive classroom. Fortunately, assessments that use videotapes of teaching and teachers' and students' work samples to evaluate what teachers actually do in the classroom have been developed by the National Board for Professional Teaching Standards (for use in certifying veteran accomplished teachers) and by states such as Connecticut for use in licensing beginning teachers. These assessments build on the knowledge base described here and have been found to be significantly related to teachers' effectiveness in producing student learning.

What policies can assure that the licensure system is made more sensible and rigorous?

• Congress should provide the funds for an independent professional authority to work with state professional standards boards and licensing authorities to develop a performance-based testing program that evaluates teaching skills for entering teachers based upon the core curriculum presented here and the successful demonstration of teaching skills in a rigorous performance assessment.

• Congress should provide incentives for states to incorporate such assessments—as well as course work and clinical requirements that reflect the knowledge and skills outlined here—into their licensing processes and to close loopholes that allow teachers to teach without meeting the standards.

In order to close these loopholes, however, it is necessary for states and the federal government to have in place incentives for recruiting an adequate supply of teachers for all communities and policies that can stem the high attrition of beginning teachers, which is the real source of most teacher shortages.

Recruitment and Retention of New Teachers

Ensuring that all teachers are well-prepared and all students have highly qualified teachers is not only a matter of improving teacher education programs. It is also a matter of ensuring that candidates who are hired have had the opportunity to experience these improved programs, that they will choose to teach where they are needed, and that they will stay in the profession and continue to grow ever more proficient. In fact, the greatest causes of teacher shortages are (1) the unequal distribution of teachers across schools, districts, and regions (with some places experiencing large surpluses while others experience shortages) and (2) the high attrition rate of beginning teachers. These attrition rates are strongly influenced by both the preservice preparation that candidates receive and the induction support they experience in their first year of teaching.

Federal and state governments can help address these problems by subsidizing candidates' studies as well as by leveraging program improvements.[7] The relevance of these investments to improved teacher education is twofold:

1. Many candidates do not get access to adequate preparation because they cannot afford either the tuition or the opportunity costs of being without employment for a period of time. And these costs are harder to bear when a recruit is entering a profession that does not promise large salaries later to compensate for loans taken earlier. Whereas many European and Asian countries completely underwrite a comprehensive program of teacher education for all candidates, the amount and quality of preparation secured by teachers in the United States is left to what they can individually afford and what programs are willing and able to offer given the resources of their respective institutions.

2. Institutions pressured to prepare working teachers who have entered teaching on emergency permits and who are trying to play catch-up with their training often water down the quality of preparation they provide. Both recruits and employers find this kind of training less satisfactory than a more coherent, supportive experience that includes supervised clinical training along with more thoughtfully organized course work.[8]

Better financial supports for teachers in training will also support the quality of training they receive—traditional or alternative. This can be accomplished by drawing in large part on the federal experience with medical manpower programs. Since 1944, the federal government has subsidized medical training to meet the needs of under-served populations, fill shortages in particular fields, and increase diversity in the medical profession. Just as is done in medicine, the federal government should provide large-scale service scholarships and forgivable loans to teachers who agree to train in shortage fields and practice in high-need locations. As in the successful North Carolina model, scholarships for high-quality teacher education can be linked to minimum service requirements of four years or more—the point at which most teachers who have remained in the classroom have committed to remaining in the profession. Some states have coupled such initiatives with subsidies for student teaching to further increase the likelihood that recruits will be able to afford to be well-prepared, rather than cutting corners to get into the classroom and then leaving quickly.

In addition, teachers are much more likely to stay in the profession if they are supported in their early efforts to learn to teach. Unlike some other professions, where new entrants are formally inducted into the profession by careful supervision, mentoring, and other apprenticeship-like experiences, teachers too often are put into a classroom and left on their own without access to more seasoned teachers or formalized ways to work through with others the difficulties of any new professional confronted with the hard realities of transforming "book knowledge" into action.

Graduation from a teacher education program—whether one year or several—cannot be considered the end of training for teachers. The demands of the precollege degree—acquiring subject-matter knowledge, pedagogical content knowledge, and clinical training—do not allow sufficient time for teacher candidates to develop the skills and experiences necessary to solve all the problems of practice they will encounter in their initial teaching assignments, including the skills necessary to work effectively with parents, colleagues, paraprofessionals and other education support staff.

Nonetheless, after graduation from a teacher education program or upon completion of an alternative route program, too many new teachers are assigned the most challenging assignments with the

largest classes, most difficult students, and most preparations and du-
ties, and then left on their own to master the intricacies of teaching.
By contrast, other countries with high-achieving school systems in-
duct new teachers into the profession through clinical, real-world
training processes—following rigorous undergraduate or graduate academic preparation—by which inductees develop and perfect their
teaching skills under the mentorship of more experienced and skilled
colleagues.

Although there has been a focus on support for beginning teachers and a call for induction programs to meet beginning teachers'
needs, existing programs vary considerably. For some teachers, induction is merely a short nuts-and-bolts orientation: for example,
where supplies are kept, where restrooms are located, and what the
school rules and procedures are. Other teachers are fortunate enough
to experience mentoring with experienced colleagues who have released time to coach them and model practices in the classroom and
who pay careful attention to the beginning teachers' developing professional practice as they confront the hard realities of the classroom.
Research has shown that effective induction programs have the following characteristics:

• *All beginning teachers are assigned qualified mentors in their teaching field who are regularly available to coach and model good instruction.*
Mentors need to be screened carefully and should meet designated criteria that ensure only high-quality practitioners assume the role. They
must be given training in mentoring and have reduced teaching loads
that allow them to go into novices' classrooms on at least a weekly
basis and have a reasonable number of new teachers to supervise.

• *Beginning teachers have reduced teaching loads.* In order to hone
their professional skills, novice teachers need both the time and the
opportunity to observe other teachers teach, plan and confer with colleagues, work with their mentors, and reflect on their own teaching.

• *The program lasts at least one year.* Research shows that when
it comes to beginning teacher induction programs, a one- to two-year
program can make the difference between a teacher who succeeds

early in her career and one who does not, and between a teacher who remains in the profession and one who does not.

* *A sound assessment of teaching skills guides the induction process and a careful review of practice completes the induction program.* Mentor teachers and principals guide and evaluate beginning teachers' performance by using professional teaching standards and assessments that examine how teachers are exhibiting the central knowledge, skills, and dispositions expected of professional teachers. Time in an induction program should not be the criteria for candidate success. Successful completion of induction should require a summative review of the candidates' teaching based on established standards of effective practice.

All beginning teachers, regardless of their pathway to certification, deserve such high-quality induction programs. What can be done to assure that quality teacher induction is a part of the beginning teacher experience?

* The federal government can provide incentives for states to develop quality teacher induction programs. Since many states and some districts have enacted some kind of induction program, some resources already are focused on these needs. Relatively few programs, however, ensure that expert mentors in the same teaching field are made available for in-classroom support, the component of induction with the greatest effect on teacher retention and learning. Part of such a program could supply grants to state agencies willing to develop statewide induction programs that would target funds to districts, universities, and other agencies to develop and test model induction programs and concentrate on support for new teachers in hard-to-staff schools.

* The states can incorporate requirements for participation in such programs as part of the licensure process, as a number of states already have done. Candidates, for example, must often complete the program and pass an embedded assessment of teaching skills in order to gain the professional license that follows the probationary period.

- States and the federal government can provide funds to districts to pay for induction programs that meet the criteria for strong programs supported by research.

A final element of retaining well-prepared teachers in schools is developing schools in which teachers can put to use the practices they have learned. Teachers are much more likely to stay if they feel they can be effective in their work. And teachers are much more likely to be trained to be effective if their clinical experiences are in schools that support good practice. If educational improvement is the goal, it is not enough to prepare individual good teachers and send them out to dysfunctional schools. If teachers are to be effective, they must work in settings in which they can use what they know—where they can come to know their students and their families well, work with other teachers to provide a coherent, well-grounded curriculum, evaluate and guide student learning by using information-rich assessments, and use texts and materials that support thoughtful learning. Unfortunately, given the hodgepodge of policies, the lack of resources in many districts, and the fragmented design of factory model schools, these conditions are absent in many U.S. schools.

Many analysts have noted that there is very little relationship between the organization of the typical American school and the demands of serious teaching and learning. This poses a much larger systemic agenda for change in schools. Given the challenges of contemporary schooling, it would be naïve to suggest that merely producing more highly skilled teachers can, by itself, dramatically change the outcomes of education. We must attend simultaneously to both sides of the reform coin: better teachers and better systems. Schools will need to continue to change to create the conditions within which powerful teaching and learning can occur, and teachers will need to be prepared to be part of this change process.

While the system changes that are needed go far beyond what individual teachers can be expected to effect, teacher preparation can support needed systemic reforms by helping teachers learn how to work on the improvement of practice as members of collaborative communities and by engaging in partnerships with schools and districts to transform schooling and teaching in tandem. In this way, prospective teachers can be prepared to teach effectively in the schools where they are needed, and they can learn first-hand how to develop contexts that will support the learning of all their students.

Many kinds of institutional commitments are also needed among organizations that sponsor teacher education: commitments to adequate funding, strong staffing of teacher education programs, improved research on program strategies and outcomes, and changes in incentive structures that discourage participation in teacher education or collaboration across parts of the university as well as between universities and schools.

In the long run, those who are concerned about the ability of all teachers to teach all students well must join their concerns about improvements within local schools and schools of education with a commitment to create policy environments that foster the development of powerful preparation for effective teaching. This will require the involvement not only of teacher educators but also of superintendents, principals, and practicing teachers who join forces to insist upon solid professional learning opportunities before and during their careers; parents and community members who understand the critical importance of investments in professional preparation for the educators of their children; university presidents, faculty, and trustees who commit to ensuring that education schools are central to the work of universities and comparable in quality to other professional schools; and policymakers who understand that if American public education is to meet the aspirations this nation has assigned to it, the preparation of excellent teachers is the central commitment without which other reforms are unlikely to succeed.

Policy Recommendations: Quick Summary

- Both traditional and alternative teacher education programs should be closely evaluated and granted accreditation only if their programs ensure that candidates master the core set of knowledge and skills described in this volume. The federal government can incorporate this expectation when it authorizes accrediting organizations.

- States should close programs that do not meet the rigorous accreditation criteria and should also refuse to grant licenses to individuals who have not successfully completed accredited programs.

- Data-tracking systems should be created to assess programs' success in preparing candidates who enter and stay in teaching and in demonstrating good practice on performance assessments.

- Teacher education programs should evaluate their programs against the recommendations proposed here and take steps to strengthen their course work and clinical work.

- States and institutions should ensure that reimbursement ratios and funding for teacher education programs are comparable to other clinically based professional programs, such as nursing and engineering.

- The federal government should provide incentives—as it does in medicine—for the development of high-quality teacher education programs in urban and poor rural communities that provide a pipeline from preparation to hiring.

- Congress should provide funds for an independent professional authority to work with state professional standards boards and licensing authorities to develop a national performance-based testing program for teachers that assesses the knowledge and skills described here through actual demonstration of teaching practice.

- Congress should provide states incentives to incorporate the assessments into their licensing processes.

- The federal government should substantially expand service scholarships and forgivable loans to subsidize education for those who prepare to teach in shortage fields and go to shortage locations, linked to minimum service requirements of four years or more.

- States and the federal government should sponsor high-quality induction programs that will help beginning teachers gain expertise and stay in the classroom. These programs should include trained mentors who are expert teachers with released time to coach and model good instruction; reduced teaching loads; and sound performance assessment to guide learning.

Notes

Introduction

1. The parent volume for this report includes the research on which this report is based. See Darling-Hammond and Bransford, LePage, Hammerness, & Duffy, 2005. It is accompanied by a companion volume, also sponsored by the National Academy of Education, that focuses on how beginning teachers should be prepared to teach reading. See Snow, Griffin, & Burns, 2005.

Chapter One

1. Bransford, Brown, & Cocking, 1999.

Chapter Two

1. Daniel Lortie called this the "apprenticeship of observation." Lortie, 1975.
2. Kennedy, 1999.
3. See for example, Chin & Russell, 1995; Denton, 1982; Denton & Lacina, 1984; Denton, Morris, & Tooke, 1982; Denton & Smith, 1983; Denton & Tooke, 1981; Sumara & Luce-Kapler, 1996.
4. McDonald, 1992.

Chapter Three

1. See for example, Darling-Hammond, 2000; Darling-Hammond & Macdonald, 2000; Hammerness, Darling-Hammond, & Shulman, 2002; Koppich, 2000; Merseth & Koppich, 2000; Miller & Silvernail, 2000; Snyder, 2000; Whitford, Ruscoe, & Fickel, 2000; Zeichner, 2000.

2. Feistritzer, 2004. See also Miller, McKenna, & McKenna, 1998; Wilson, Floden, & Ferrini-Mundy, 2001.

3. See, for example, National Commission on Teaching and America's Future, 1996.

4. See, for example, Frey, 2002; Gettys et al., 1999; Gill & Hove, 1999; Glaeser, Karge, Smith, & Weatherill, 2002; Mantle-Bromley, 2002; Neubert & Binko, 1998; Sandholz & Dadlez, 2000; Shroyer et al., 1996; Stallings, Bossung, & Martin, 1990; Trachtman, 1996; Wiseman & Cooner, 1996; Yerian & Grossman, 1997.

5. Darling-Hammond & Hammerness, 2002.

Chapter Four

1. See Hanushek, Kain, & Rivkin, 1998; see also Kain & Singleton, 1996.

2. Benner, 2000.

3. Henke, Chen, Geis, & Knepper, 2000. See also National Commission on Teaching and America's Future, 2003; Luczak, 2004.

4. See Bond, Jaeger, Smith, & Hattie, 2001; Goldhaber & Anthony, 2004; Vandevoort, Amrein-Beardsley, & Berliner, 2004 for studies on the effectiveness of National Board Certified teachers.

5. Title 42, chapter 6A, subchapter V of the U.S. Code details the many components of this system.

6. See American Federation of Teachers, 2000; Haertel, 1991; Porter, Youngs, & Odden, 2001.

7. For further description of policies mentioned in this section for attracting and retaining teachers, see Darling-Hammond & Sykes, 2003.

8. See California State University, 2002; Shields et al., 2001.

Bibliography

American Federation of Teachers. (2000). *Building a profession: Strengthening teacher preparation and induction, a report of the K–16 Teacher Education Task Force.* Washington, DC: Author.

Benner, A. D. (2000). *The cost of teacher turnover.* Austin, TX: Texas Center for Educational Research.

Bond, L., Jaeger, R., Smith, T., & Hattie, J. (2001). Defrocking the National Board: The certification system of the National Board for Professional Teaching Standards. *Education Matters, 1*(2), 79–82.

Bransford, J. D., Brown, A. L., & Cocking, R. R. (Eds.). (1999). *How people learn: Brain, mind, experiences, and school.* Washington, DC: National Academy of Sciences Press.

California State University. (2002). *First system wide evaluation of teacher education programs in the California State University: Summary report.* Long Beach: Office of the Chancellor, California State University.

Chin, P., & Russell, T. (1995, June). *Structure and coherence in a teacher education program: Addressing the tension between systematics and the educative agenda.* Paper presented at the Annual Meeting of the Canadian Society for the Study of Education, Montreal, Quebec, Canada.

Darling-Hammond, L. (Ed.). (2000). *Studies of excellence in teacher education* (3 volumes). Washington, DC: American Association of Colleges for Teacher Education.

Darling-Hammond, L., Bransford, J. D., LePage, P., Hammerness, K., & Duffy, H. (Eds.). (2005). *Preparing teachers for a changing world: What teachers should learn and be able to do.* San Francisco: Jossey-Bass.

Darling-Hammond, L., & Hammerness, K. (2002). Toward a pedagogy of cases in teacher education. *Teaching Education, 13*(2), 125–135.

Darling-Hammond, L., & MacDonald, M. (2000). Where there is learning there is hope: The preparation of teachers at the Bank Street College of Education. In L. Darling-Hammond (Ed.), *Studies of excellence in teacher education: Preparation at the graduate level* (pp. 1–95). Washington, DC: American Association of Colleges for Teacher Education.

Darling-Hammond, L., & Sykes, G. (2003). Wanted: A national teacher supply policy for education: The right way to meet the 'highly qualified teacher' challenge. *Educational Policy Analysis Archives, 11*(33). *http://epaa.asu.edu/epaa/v11n33/.*

Denton, J. J. (1982). Early field experience influence on performance in subsequent coursework. *Journal of Teacher Education, 33*(2), 19–23.

Denton, J. J., & Lacina, L. J. (1984). Quantity of professional education coursework linked with process measures of student teaching. *Teacher Education and Practice, 39–64.*

Denton, J. J., Morris, J. E., & Tooke, D. J. (1982). The influence of academic characteristics of student teachers on the cognitive attainment of learners. *Educational and Psychological Research, 2*(1), 15–29.

Denton, J. J., & Smith, N. L. (1983). *Alternative teacher preparation programs: A cost-effectiveness comparison.* Research on Evaluation Program, Paper and Report Series No. 86. Eugene: University of Oregon.

Denton, J. J., & Tooke, D. J. (1981). Examining learner cognitive attainment as a basis for assessing student teachers. *Action in Teacher Education, 3*(4), 39–45.

Feistritzer, E. (2004). *Alternative teacher certification: A state-by-state analysis.* Washington, DC: National Center for Education Information.

Flexner, A., & Pritchett, H. S. (1910). *Medical education in the United States and Canada: A report to the Carnegie Foundation for the Advancement of Teaching.* New York: Carnegie Foundation for the Advancement of Teaching.

Frey, N. (2002). Literacy achievement in an urban middle-level professional development school: A learning community at work. *Reading Improvement, 39*(1), 3–13.

Gettys, C. M., Puckett, K., Ray, B. M., Rutledge, V. C., Stepanske, J., & University of Tennessee-Chattanooga. (1999). *The professional development school experience evaluation.* Paper presented at Mid-South Educational Research Association Conference, Gatlinburg, TN.

Gill, B., & Hove, A. (1999). *The Benedum collaborative model of teacher education: A preliminary evaluation.* Report prepared for the Benedum Center for Education Reform DB-303-EDU. Santa Monica, CA: Rand Education.

Glaeser, B. C., Karge, B. D., Smith, J., & Weatherill, C. (2002). Paradigm pioneers: A professional development school collaborative for special education teacher education candidates. In I. N. Guadarrama, J. Ramsey, & J. L. Nath (Eds.), *Forging alliances in community and thought: Research in professional development schools* (pp. 125–152). Greenwich, CT: Information Age Publishing.

Goldhaber, D., & Anthony, E. (2004). Can teacher quality be effectively assessed? Seattle, WA: Center on Reinventing Public Education, Daniel J. Evans School of Public Affairs, University of Washington. Retrieved March 22, 2004, from http://www.crpe.org/workingpapers/pdf/NBPTSquality_report.pdf.

Grossman, P., & Schoenfeld, A. (2005). Teaching subject matter. In L. Darling-Hammond, J. D. Bransford, P. LePage, K. Hammerness, & H. Duffy (Eds.), *Preparing teachers for a changing world: What teachers should learn and be able to do* (pp. 201–231). San Francisco: Jossey-Bass.

Haertel, E. H. (1991). New forms of teacher assessment. *Review of Research in Education, 17,* 3–29.

Hammerness, K., Darling-Hammond, L., & Shulman, L. (2002). *Towards expert thinking: How case-writing contributes to the development of theory-based professional knowledge in student-teachers.* Paper presented at the Annual Meeting of the American Educational Research Association, April 10–14, Seattle, WA.

Hanushek, E., Kain, J., & Rivkin, S. (1998). *Teachers, schools, and academic achievement. (Working paper 6691).* Cambridge MA: National Bureau of Economic Research.

Henke, R. R., Chen, X., Geis, S. & Knepper, P. (2000). *Progress through the teacher pipeline: 1992–93 college graduates and elementary/secondary school teaching as of 1997.* NCES 2000–152. Washington, DC: National Center for Education Statistics.

Kain, J., & Singleton, K. (1996). Equality of educational opportunity revisited. *New England Economic Review* (May, June), 87–111.

Kennedy, M. (1999). The role of preservice teacher education. In L. Darling-Hammond & G. Sykes (Eds.), *Teaching as the learning profession: Handbook of policy and practice* (pp. 54–85). San Francisco: Jossey-Bass.

Koppich, J. (2000). Trinity University: Preparing teachers for tomorrow's schools. In L. Darling-Hammond (Ed.), *Studies of excellence in teacher education: Preparation in a five-year program* (pp. 1–48). Washington, DC: American Association of Colleges for Teacher Education.

Lortie, D. C. (1975). *Schoolteacher: A sociological study.* Chicago: University of Chicago Press.

Luczak, J. (2004). *Who will teach in the 21st century? Beginning teacher training experiences and attrition rates.* Unpublished doctoral dissertation, Stanford University, Stanford, CA.

Mantle-Bromley, C. (2002). The status of early theories of professional development school potential. In I. Guadarrama, J. Ramsey, & J. Nath (Eds.), *Forging alliances in community and thought: Research in professional development schools* (pp. 3–30). Greenwich, CT: Information Age Publishing.

McDonald, J. P. (1992). *Teaching: Making sense of an uncertain craft.* New York: Teachers College Press.

Merseth, K. K., & Koppich, J. (2000). Teacher education at the University of Virginia: A study of English and mathematics preparation. In L. Darling-Hammond (Ed.), *Studies of excellence in teacher education: Preparation in a five-year program* (pp. 49–81). Washington, DC: American Association of Colleges for Teacher Education Publications.

Miller, J. W., McKenna, M. C., & McKenna, B. A. (1998). A comparison of alternatively and traditionally prepared teachers. *Journal of Teacher Education, 49*(3), 165–176.

Miller, L., & Silvernail, D. L. (2000). Learning to become a teacher: The Wheelock way. In L. Darling-Hammond (Ed.), *Studies of excellence in teacher education: Preparation in the undergraduate years* (pp. 67–107). Washington, DC: American Association of Colleges for Teacher Education Publications.

National Commission on Teaching and America's Future. (1996). *What matters most: Teaching for America's future.* New York: Author.

National Commission on Teaching and America's Future (2003). *No dream denied: A pledge to America's children.* Washington, DC: Author.

Neubert, G., & Binko, J. (1998). Professional development schools—The proof is in the performance. *Educational Leadership, 55*(5), 44–46.

Porter, A. C., Youngs, P., & Odden, A. (2001). Advances in teacher assessments and their uses. In V. Richardson (Ed.), *Handbook of research on teaching* (4th ed.) (pp. 259–297). Washington, DC: American Educational Research Association.

Sandholtz, J. H., & Dadlez, S. H. (2000). Professional development school trade-offs in teacher preparation and renewal. *Teacher Education Quarterly, 27*(1), 7–27.

Shields, P. M., Humphrey, D. C., Wechsler, M. E., Riel, L. M., Tiffany-Morales, J., Woodworth, K., et al. (2001). *The status of the teaching profession 2001.* Santa Cruz, CA: The Center for the Future of Teaching and Learning.

Shroyer, G. M., Wright, E. L., & Ramey-Gasser, L. (1996). An innovative model for collaborative reform in elementary school science teaching. *Journal of Science Teacher Education, 7*(3), 151–168.

Snow, C., Griffin, P., & Burns, S. (2005). *Knowledge to support the teaching of reading: Preparing teachers for a changing world.* San Francisco: Jossey-Bass.

Snyder, J. (1999). *New Haven Unified School District: A teaching quality system for excellence and equity.* Washington DC: National Commission on Teaching and America's Future.

Snyder, J. (2000). Knowing children—understanding teaching: The developmental teacher education program at the University of California, Berkeley. In L. Darling-Hammond (Ed.), *Studies of excellence in teacher education: Preparation at the graduate level* (pp. 97–172). Washington, DC: American Association of Colleges for Teacher Education.

Stallings, J., Bossung, J., & Martin, A. (1990). Houston Teaching Academy: Partnership in developing teachers. *Teaching and Teacher Education, 6*(4), 355–365.

Sumara, D. J., & Luce-Kapler, R. (1996). (Un)Becoming a teacher: Negotiating identities while learning to teach. *Canadian Journal of Education, 21*(1), 65–83.

Trachtman, R. (1996). *The NCATE professional development school study: A survey of 28 PDS sites*. Unpublished manuscript. (Available from Professional Development School Standards Project, National Council for Accreditation of Teacher Education, Washington, DC 20036.)

Vandevoort, L. G., Amrein-Beardsley, A., and Berliner, D. (2004). National board certified teachers and their students' achievement. *Educational Policy Analysis Archives, 12*(46). Retrieved November 8, 2004, from http://epaa.asu.edu/epaa/v12n46/.

Whitford, B. L., Ruscoe, G. C., & Fickel, L. (2000). Knitting it all together: Collaborative teacher education in Southern Maine. In L. Darling-Hammond (Ed.), *Studies of excellence in teacher education: Preparation at the graduate level* (pp. 173–257). Washington, DC: American Association of Colleges for Teacher Education.

Wilson, S. M., Floden, R. E., & Ferrini-Mundy, J. (2001). *Teacher preparation research: Current knowledge, gaps, and recommendations: A research report prepared for the U.S. Department of Education*. Seattle, WA: Center for the Study of Teaching and Policy.

Wiseman, D. L., & Cooner, D. (1996). Discovering the power of collaboration: The impact of a school-university partnership on teaching. *Teacher Education and Practice 12*(1), 18–28.

Yerian, S., & Grossman, P. L. (1997). Preservice teachers' perceptions of their middle level teacher education experience: A comparison of a traditional and a PDS Model. *Teacher Education Quarterly, 24*(4), 85–101.

Zeichner, K. M. (2000). Ability-based teacher education: Elementary teacher education at Alverno College. In L. Darling-Hammond, (Ed.), *Studies of excellence in teacher education: Preparation in the undergraduate years* (pp. 1–66). Washington, DC: American Association of Colleges for Teacher Education Publications.

About the Editors

Linda Darling-Hammond is the Charles E. Ducommun Professor of Education at Stanford University, where she has served since 1998 as faculty sponsor for the Stanford Teacher Education Program. Darling-Hammond is also co-director of the Stanford Educational Leadership Institute and the School Redesign Network. She was the founding executive director of the National Commission for Teaching and America's Future, the blue-ribbon panel whose 1996 report, *What Matters Most: Teaching for America's Future*, catalyzed major policy changes across the United States to improve the quality of teacher education and teaching. Her research, teaching, and policy work focus on issues of teaching quality, school reform, and educational equity. Among her more than two hundred publications are *Teaching as the Learning Profession* (co-edited with Gary Sykes), recipient of the National Staff Development Council's Outstanding Book Award for 2000, and *The Right to Learn*, recipient of the American Educational Research Association's Outstanding Book Award for 1998.

Joan Baratz-Snowden is director of Educational Issues at the American Federation of Teachers (AFT). In that capacity, she oversees the department's work related to publications, the technical assistance and other services it provides to members, and the dissemination to the public of AFT's policies on professional issues such as standards and assessments, reading, teacher quality, and redesign of schools to raise achievement. Prior to joining the AFT, Baratz-Snowden was vice president for Education Policy and Reform and for Assessment and Research at the National Board for Professional Teaching Standards

(NBPTS). She was responsible for addressing policy issues related to creating a more effective school environment for teaching and learning, increasing the supply of high-quality entrants to teaching, improving teacher education and continuing professional development, and directing the initial research and development activities necessary to develop the NBPTS assessments. Baratz-Snowden also directed the Education Policy Research and Services Division at the Educational Testing Service. She is well known for her policy studies in the politics of testing and evaluation. Her research examined issues of the impact and use of standardized testing in schools, colleges, and universities and the entrance to teaching and other professions.

Index

Other Books of Interest

Preparing Teachers for a Changing World:
What Teachers Should Learn and Be Able to Do

Linda Darling-Hammond, John Bransford

Cloth ISBN: 0-7879-7464-1

www.josseybass.com

"The knowledge base for teacher preparation and teaching is maturing and becoming very relevant to practice. This state-of-the-art compendium is essential reading for teacher educators committed to preparing professionals who can teach so that all children will, in fact, learn." —*Arthur E. Wise, president, National Council for Accreditation of Teacher Education*

Based on rapid advances in what is known about how people learn and how to teach effectively, this important book examines the core concepts and central pedagogies that should be at the heart of any teacher education program. Stemming from the results of a commission sponsored by the National Academy of Education, *Preparing Teachers for a Changing World* recommends the creation of an informed teacher education curriculum with the common elements that represent state-of-the-art standards for the profession.

Written for teacher educators in both traditional and alternative programs, university and school system leaders, teachers, staff development professionals, researchers, and educational policymakers, the book addresses the key foundational knowledge for teaching and discusses how to implement that knowledge within the classroom. *Preparing Teachers for a Changing World* recommends that, in addition to strong subject matter knowledge, all new teachers have a basic understanding of how people learn and develop, as well as how children acquire and use language, which is the currency of education. In addition, the book suggests that teaching professionals must be able to apply that knowledge in developing curriculum that attends to students' needs, the demands of the content, and the social purposes of education: in teaching specific subject matter to diverse students, in managing the classroom, assessing student performance, and using technology in the classroom.

The ideas and suggestions outlined in this book have far-reaching implications for educational policy, classroom practice, and staff development and will go a long way toward informing the next generation of teachers.

Linda Darling-Hammond is the Charles E. Ducommun Professor of Education at Stanford University and executive director of the National Commission on Teaching and America's Future. She lives in Stanford, California with her husband and three children.

John D. Bransford is Centenniel Professor of Psychology and Education and co-director of the Learning Technology Center at Vanderbilt University. He is co-chair of the National Academy of Education's Committee on Teacher Education.

Collaborating editors Pamela LePage, Karen Hammerness, and Helen Duffy served as staff of the National Academy's Committee on Teacher Education.

Knowledge to Support the
Teaching of Reading
Preparing Teachers for a Changing World

Catherine Snow, Peg Griffin,
M. Susan Burns, *Editors*

Cloth ISBN: 0-7879-7465-X

www.josseybass.com

While it's now recognized that basic reading proficiency is key to student success in all content areas, many teachers have not been specifically grounded in the fundamentals of reading theory and practice, especially if their area of expertise is in another discipline.

This book presents recommendations for the essential knowledge new teachers need to know about the development, acquisition, and teaching of language and literacy skills. This volume is the first to offer recommendations for this core knowledge base from the esteemed National Academy of Education.

Knowledge to Support the Teaching of Reading will become the definitive guide to reading and literacy preparation for teacher education, and its recommendations will be widely adopted. Whether you are a classroom teacher, reading specialist, teacher educator, staff developer, or an educational administrator, you will find Catherine Snow's recommendations relevant and essential to your professional development and those with whom you work.

Catherine Snow is the Henry Lee Shattuck professor of education at the Harvard Graduate School of Education. She is an expert on language and literacy development in children, focusing on how oral language skills are acquired and how they relate to literacy outcomes. She has recently chaired two national panels for the National Academy of Sciences and the Rand Reading Study Group.

Also Sponsored by the National Academy of Education